CONTENTS.

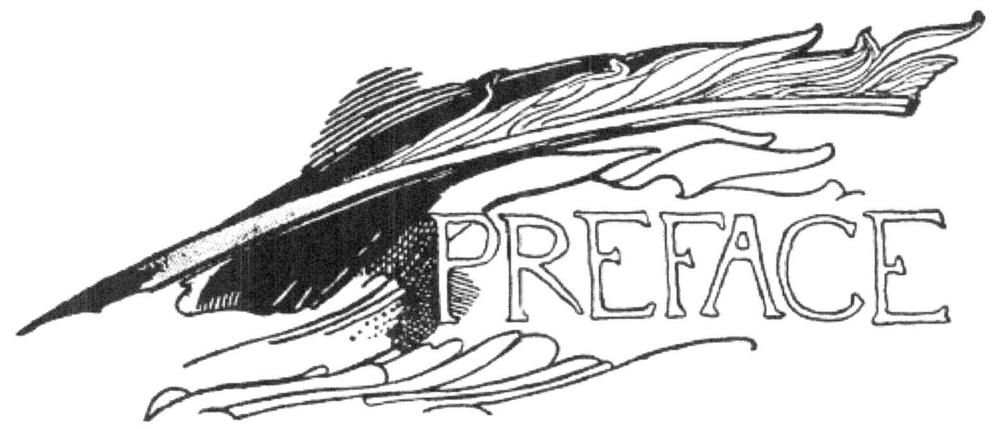

Everywhere to-day is the Illustrator (artist he may not always be), for never was illustration so marketable as now; and the correspondence-editors of the Sunday papers have at length found a new outlet for the superfluous energies of their eager querists in advising them to "go in" for black and white: as one might advise an applicant to adventure upon a commercial enterprise of large issues and great risks before the amount of his capital (if any) had been ascertained.

It is so very easy to make black marks upon white cardboard, is it not? and not particularly difficult to seize upon the egregious mannerisms of the accepted purveyors of "the picturesque"—that *cliché* phrase, battered nowadays out of all real meaning.

But for really serious art—personal, aggressive, definite and instructed —one requires something more than a *penchant*, or the stimulating impulsion of an empty pocket, or even the illusory magnetism of the *vie bohême* of the lady-novelist, whose artists still wear velvet coats and aureoles of auburn hair, and marry the inevitable heiress in the third volume. Not that one really wishes to be one of those creatures, for the lady-novelists' love-lorn embryonic Michael Angelos are generally great cads; but this by the way!

What is wanted in the aspirant is the vocation: the feeling for beauty of line and for decoration, and the powers both of idealizing and of selection. Pen-drawing and allied methods are the chiefest means of illustration at this day, and these qualities are essential to their successful employ.

Practitioners in pen-and-ink are already numerous enough to give any new-comer pause before he adds himself to their number, but certainly the greater number of them are merely journalists without sense of style; mannerists only of a peculiarly vicious parasitic type.

"But," ask those correspondents, "does illustration pay?" "Yes," says that omniscient person, the Correspondence-Editor. Then those pixie-led wayfarers through life, filled with an inordinate desire to draw, to paint, to translate Nature on to canvas or cardboard (at a profit), set about the staining of fair paper, the wasting of good ink, brushes, pens, and all the materials with which the graphic arts are pursued, and lo! just because the greater number of them set out, not with the love of an art, but with the single idea of a paying investment of time and labour—it does *not* pay! Remuneration in their case is Latin for three farthings.

Publishers and editors, it is said, can now, with the cheapness of modern methods of reproduction as against the expense of wood-engraving, afford to pay artists better because they pay engravers less. Perhaps they can. But do they?

Pen-drawing in particular has, by reason of these things, almost come to stand for exaggeration and a shameless license—a convention that sees and renders everything in a manner flamboyantly quaint. But this vein is being worked down to the bed-rock: it has plumbed its deepest depth, and everything now points to a period of instructed sobriety where now the untaught *abandon* of these mannerists has rioted through the pages of illustrated magazines and newspapers to a final disrepute.

Artists are now beginning to ask how they can dissociate themselves from that merely manufacturing army of frantic draughtsmen who never, or rarely, go beyond the exercise of pure line-work; and the widening power of process gives them answer. Results striking and unhackneyed are always to be obtained to-day by those who are not hag-ridden by that purely Philistine ideal of the clear sharp line.

These pages are written as a plea for something else than the eternal round of uninspired work. They contain suggestions and examples of results obtained in striving to be at one with modern methods of reproduction, and perhaps I may be permitted to hope that in this direction they may be of some service.

INTRODUCTORY.

Pen-drawing is the most spontaneous of the arts, and amongst the applied crafts the most modern. The professional pen-draughtsman was unknown but a few years since; fifteen years ago, or thereabouts, he was an obscure individual, working at a poorly considered craft, and handling was so seldom thought of that the illustrator who could draw passably well was rarely troubled by his publisher on the score of technique. For that which had deserved the name of technique was dead, so far as illustration was concerned, and "process," which was presently to vivify it, was, although born already, but yet a sickly child. To-day the illustrators are numerous beyond computation, and the name of those who are impelled to the spoiling of good paper and the wasting of much ink is indeed legion.

For uncounted years before the invention of photo-mechanical methods of engraving, there had been practised a method of drawing with the pen, which formed a pretty pastime wherewith to fleet the idle hours of the gentlemanly amateur, and this was, for no discoverable reason, called "etching."

It is needless at this time to go into the derivatives of that word, with the object of proving that the verb "to etch" means something very different from drawing in ink with a pen; it should have, long since, been demonstrated to everybody's satisfaction that etching is the art of drawing on metal with a point, and of biting in that drawing with acids. But the manufacturers of pens long fostered the fallacy by selling so-called etching-pens: probably they do so even now.

By whom pen-drawings were first called etchings none can say. Certainly the two arts have little or nothing in common: the terms are not interchangeable. Etching has its own especial characteristics, which may, to an extent, be imitated with the pen, but the quality and direction of line produced by a rigid steel point on metal are entirely different from the lines drawn with a flexible nib upon paper. The line produced by an etching needle has a uniform thickness, but with the needle you can work in any imaginable direction upon the copper plate. With a nib upon paper, a line varying in thickness with the pressure of the hand results, but there is not that entirely free use of the hand as with the etching point: you cannot with entire freedom draw from and toward yourself.

The greatest exponents of pen-drawing have not entirely conquered the normal inability of the pen to express the infinite delightful waywardnesses of the etching-point. Again, the etched line is only less sharp than the line made by the graver upon wood; the line drawn with the pen upon the smoothest surface is ragged, viewed under a magnifying glass. This, of course, is not a plea for a clean line in pen-work—that is only the ideal of commercial draughtsmanship—but the man who can produce such a line with the pen at will, who can overcome the tendency to inflexible lines, has risen victorious over the stubbornness of a material.

The sketch-books, gilt-lettered and india-rubber banded, of the bread-and-butter miss, and what one may be allowed, perhaps, to term the "pre-process" amateur generally, give no hint of handling, no foretaste of technique. They are barren of aught save ill-registered facts, and afford no pleasure to the eye, which is the end, the sensuous end, of all art. Rather did these artless folk almost invariably seek to adventure beyond the province of the pen by strokes infinitely little and microscopic, so that they might haply deceive the eye by similarity to wood engravings or steel prints. But in those days pen-drawing was only a pursuit; to-day it is a living art. Now, an art is not merely a storehouse of facts, nor a moral influence. If it was of these things, then the photographic camera would be all-powerful, and all that would be left to do with the hands would be the production of devotional pictures; and of those who produced them the best artist would infallibly be him with a character the most noted for piety. Art, to the contrary, is entirely independent of subject or morals. It is not sociology, nor ever shall be; and those who practise an art might be the veriest pariahs, and yet their works rank technically, artistically, among the best. Art is handling *in excelsis*, and its results lie properly in the pride of the eye and the satisfaction of the æsthetic sense, though Mr. Ruskin would have it otherwise.

Is this the lashing of a dead horse, or thrice slaying the slain? No, I think not. The moral and literary fallacies remain. Open an art exhibition and give your exhibits technical, not subject titles, and you shall hear a mighty howl, I promise you. Mr. Hamerton, too, has recently found grudging occasion to say that, for artists, "it does not appear that a literary education would be necessary in all cases." Whenever was it necessary? But then Mr. Hamerton is himself one of those philosophic writers of a winning literary turn who can practise an art in by no means a distinguished way, but who write dogma by the yard and fumble over every illustration of their precepts. His *Drawing and Engraving*—a reprint from his *Encyclopædia Britannica* article—is worse than useless to the student of illustration, and especially of pen-drawing, because Mr. Hamerton has long been left behind the times. He knows little of the admirable modern methods of reproducing line-work, but gives us etymologies of drawing and historical dissertations on engraving, which we do not want. Of such antiquated matter are even the current editions of encyclopædias fashioned. The fact is, the bulk of art criticism is written by men who can only string platitudes and stale studio slang together, without beginning to understand principles. The appalling journalese of much "art criticism" is hopelessly out of date; the slang of a half-forgotten *atélier* is the lingo of would-be criticism to-day.

It seems strange that a man who can write pretty *vers de société* or another who writes essays (essays, truly, in the philological sense), should for such acquirements be amongst those to whom is delegated the criticism of art in painting, drawing, or engraving; but so it is. No one who has not surmounted the difficulties of a medium can truly appreciate technique in it, whether that medium be words, or paint, or ink. No one, for instance, would give a painter or a pen-artist the chance to review a poet's new volume of poems. You would not send a plumber to pronounce upon a baker's method of kneading his dough. No; but an ordinary reporter is judged capable of criticizing a gallery of pictures. You cannot get much artistic change out of his report, nor from the articles on art written by a man whose only claim to the standing of "art critic" is the possession of a second-class certificate in drawing from the Science and Art Department. But of such stuff are the neurotic Neros of the literary "art critique" fashioned, and equally unauthorized by works are the lectures on illustration with which the ingenious Mr. Blackburn at decent intervals tickles suburban audiences or the amiable *dilettante* of the Society of Arts into the fallacious belief that they know all about it, "which," to quote the Euclidian formula, "is absurd." Indeed, not even the most industrious, the best-informed, nor the most catholic-minded man could ever lecture, or write articles, or publish an illustrated critical work upon illustration which should show an approximation to completeness in its examples of styles and methods. The thing has been attempted, but will never be done, because the quantity of work—even good work—that has been produced is so vast, the styles so varied. The great storehouses of the best pen-work are the magazines, and from them the eclectic will gather a rich harvest. The *Century* and *Harper's* are now the chief of these. The *Magazine of Art* and the *Portfolio*, which were used to be filled with good original work, are now busied in providing such *réchauffés* as photographic blocks from paintings old and new, but chiefly old, because they cost nothing for copyright. As for newspaper work, the *Daily Graphic* is creating a school of its own, which does far better work than ever its New York namesake (now defunct) ever printed.

Some beautiful and most suggestive pen-drawings are to be found in the earlier numbers of *L'Art* and many Parisian publications, such as the *Courier Français*, *Vie Moderne*, *Paris Illustré*, and *La Petit Journal pour Rire*. Many of the *Salon* catalogues, too, contain admirable examples.

THE RISE OF AN ART.

Photo-mechanical processes of reproduction were invented by men who sought, not to create an art, not to help art in any way, but only to cheapen the cost of reproduction. "Line" processes—that is to say, processes for the reproduction of pure line—though not the first invented amongst modern methods, were the first to come into a state of practical utility; though even then their results were so crude that the artists whom necessity led to draw for them sank at once to a deeper depth than ever they had sounded when the *fac-simile* wood-cutter held them in bondage. They became the slaves of mechanical limitations and chemical formulæ, which was a worse condition than having been henchmen of a craftsman. So far as the æsthetic sense is concerned, the process illustration of previous date to (say) 1880 might all be destroyed and no harm done, save, perhaps, the loss of much evidence of a documentary character toward the history of early days of processes.

There have been two great factors in their gradual perfection—competition with the wood-engravers and of rival process firms one with another, and, perhaps more important still, the independency of a few artists who have found methods of drawing with the pen, and have followed them despite the temporary limitations of the process-man. The workmen have "drawn for process" in the worst and most commercial sense of the term; they have set down their lines after the hard-and-fast rules which were formulated for their guidance. For years after the invention of zincography, artists who were induced to make drawings for the new methods of engraving worked in a dull round of routine; for in those days the process-man was not less, but more, tyrannical than his predecessor, the wood-engraver; his yoke was, for a time, harder to bear.

One was enjoined to make drawings with only the blackest of Indian ink, upon Bristol-board, the thickest and smoothest and whitest that could be obtained, and upon none other. It was impressed upon the draughtsman that he should draw lines thick and wide apart and firm, and that his drawings should be made with a view to, preferably, a reduction in scale of one-third. Also that by no means should his lines run together by any chance, except in the matter of a coarse and obvious cross-hatch. And so, by reason of these things, the pen-work of that time is become dreadful to look upon at this day. The man who then drew with a view to reproduction squirmed on the very edge of his chair, and with compressed lips, and his heart in his mouth, drew upon his Bristol-board slowly and carefully, and with so heavy a hand, that presently his wrist ached consumedly, and his drawing became stilted in the extreme. Not yet was pen-drawing a profession, for few men had learned these formulæ; and the zincography of that time made miserable all them that were translated by it into something appreciably different from their original work. Illustration, although already sensibly increased in volume, was artistically at the lowest ebb. It was a manufacture, an industry; but scarcely a profession, and most certainly it had not yet become an art.

When technique in drawing for process began to appear as an individual technique opposed to the old *fac-simile* wood-engraving needs, it was a handling entirely abominable and inartistic. If old-time drawing for the wood-engravers was pursued in grooves of convention, working for the zincographer proceeded in ruts. There have never been, before or since, such horribly uninspired things produced as in the first years of process-work in these islands. Such dull, scratchy, spotty, wiry-looking prints resulted: they were, as now, produced in zinc, and they proclaimed it unmistakably. Had not these new methods been about one-fifth the cost of wood-engraving, they would have had no chance whatever. But we are a commercial and an inartistic people, and publishers, careless of appearance, welcomed any results that gave them a typographic block at a fifth of its former cost.

Process, in its beginnings, was not a promising method of reproduction. Men saw scarcely anything in it save cheap (and nasty) ways of multiplying diagrams, and the bald and generally artless elevations of new buildings issued from architects' offices. But in course of time, better blocks, with practice, became possible, and freer use of the pen was obtained; although at every unhackneyed stroke the process-man shrieked disaster. It is incalculable how much time has been wasted, how many careers set back, by obedience to the hard-and-fast rules laid down for the guidance of artists by the process-people of years since. To those artists who, with an artistic recklessness of results entirely admirable and praiseworthy, set down their work as they pleased, we owe, more than to any others, the progress of process; by their immediate martyrdom was our eventual salvation earned. And in the sure and certain hope of a reproduction really and truly *fac-simile*, the draughtsman in the medium of pen-and-ink is to-day become a technician of a peculiar subtlety.

To-day, with the exercise of knowledge and discrimination, drawings the most difficult of reproduction may be rendered faithfully; it is a matter only of choice of processes. But in the mass of reproduction at this time, this knowledge, this discrimination, are often seen to be lacking. It is a matter of commerce, of course, for a publisher, an editor, to send off originals in bulk to one firm, and to await from one source the resulting blocks. But unknowing, or reckless of their individual merits and needs, our typical editor has thus consigned some drawings to an unkind fate. There are many processes even for the reproduction of line, and drawings of varying characteristics are better reproduced by different methods; they should each be sent for reproduction on its own merits.

It was in 1884 that there began to arise quite a number of original styles in pen-work, and then this new profession was by way of becoming an art. You will not find any English-printed book or magazine before this date showing a sign of this new art, but now it arose suddenly, and at once became an irresponsible, unreasoning welter of ill-considered mannerisms. Ever since 1884, until within the last year or two, pen-draughtsmen have rioted through every conceivable and inconceivable vagary of manner. The artists who by force of artistry and character have helped to spur on the process-man against his will, and have worked with little or no heed to the shortcomings of his science, have freed the hands of a dreadful rabble that has revelled merely in eccentricity. Thus has liberty for a space meant a licence so wild that to-day it has become quite refreshing to turn back to the sobriety of the old illustrators of from thirty to forty years ago, who drew for the *fac-simile* wood-engraver.

From 1857, through the '60's, and on to 1875, when it finally shredded out, there existed a fine convention in drawing for illustration and the wood-engraver. Among the foremost exponents of it were Millais, Sandys, Charles Green, Robert Barnes, Simeon Solomon, Mahony, J. D. Watson, and J. D. Linton. Pinwell and Fred Walker, too, produced excellent work in this manner, before they untimely died.

The *Sunday Magazine, Once a Week, Good Words, Cornhill,* the first two years of the *Graphic,* and, where the drawings have not been drawn down to their humourous legends, the volumes of *Punch* during this period, are a veritable storehouse of beautiful examples of this peculiarly English school. It was a convention that grew out of the wood-engraver's imposed limits, and they became transcended by the art of the young artists of that day.

There is a certain sweetness and grace in those old illustrations that seems to increase with the widening of that gulf between our day and the day of their production. It is not for the sake of their draughtsmanship alone (though that is excellent), but chiefly for their technical qualities, and their fine character-drawing, that those monumental achievements in illustration appeal so strongly to the artistic eye to-day. We have been accustomed during these last years to the stress of mannerism, the *bravura* treatment of imported art, bringing with it strange atmospheres which have nothing in common with our duller skies, and, truth to tell, we want a change. Now, we might do much worse than hark back to the '60's, and study the peculiar style brought about by the needs of the wood-engraver, but transformed into an admirable school by men who wrought their trammels into a convention so great that it cannot fail, some day, to be revived.

It is greatly to be deplored that we have not left to us the original drawings of that time and these men. In the majority of cases, and through a long series of years, the drawings from which these *fac-simile* wood-engravings were made were drawn by the artists on the wood block, and engraved, so that we have left to us only the more or less successful engraver's imitation of the artists' original line-work. But when these blocks were the work of the Dalziels, or of Swain, we may generally take them as a close approximation to the original drawing. Pen and pencil both were used upon the wood blocks: some of these are to be seen at the South Kensington Museum, with the original drawings upon them still uncut, photography having in the mean while become applied to the use of transferring a drawing from paper to the wood surface.

Unless you have practised etching on copper, in which you have to draw upon the plate in reverse, you can have little idea of the relief experienced by the artists of thirty years ago, when the necessity for drawing in reverse upon the wood was obviated.

Now, I am not going to say that with pen and ink and process-reproduction you could obtain the sweetness of the wood-engraved line, but something of it should be possible, and the dignified, almost classic, reserve and repose of this style of draughtsmanship could be, in great measure, brought back to help assuage the worry of the ultra-clever pen-work of to-day, and to form a grateful relief from that peculiarly modern vice in illustration, of "making a hole in the page."

The great difficulty that would lie in the way of such a revival would be that those who would attempt it would need to be good draughtsmen; and of these there are not many. No tricks nor flashy treatment hid bad drawing in this technique, as in much of the slap-dashiness of to-day. And not only would sound draughtsmanship be essential, but also characterization of a peculiarly well-seen and graphic description. The illustrator of a generation ago worked under tremendous disadvantages. "Phiz" etched his inimitable illustrations of Dickens upon steel with all the attendant drawbacks of working in reverse, yet he would be a bold man or reckless who should decry him. He was, at his best, greater beyond comparison than THE Cruickshank—George, in the forefront of that artistic trinity—and he reached his highest point in the delightful composition of "Captain Cuttle consoles his Friend," in *DombeyandSon* . Composition and characterization are beyond anything done before or since. It is distinctly, obviously, great, and it fits the author and his story like—like a glove. One cannot find a newer and better simile than that for good fitting. And (not to criticize modern work severely *because* it is modern) the greater bulk of illustration to-day fits the stories it professes to elucidate like a Strand tailor.

There are facilities now for buying electrotypes from magazines and illustrated periodicals, by which engravings that have already served one turn in illustrating a story can be purchased, to do duty again in illustrating another; and this is a practice very widely prevalent to-day. And why can this be so readily done? The answer is near to seek. It is because illustration is become so characterless that it is so readily interchangeable. Perhaps it may be sought to lay the blame upon the author; and certainly there is not at this time so ready a field for character-drawing as Dickens presented. But I have not seen any illustrations to Mr. Hardy's tales, nor to Mr. Stevenson's, that realize the excellently well-shown types in their works.

If you should chance to see any early volumes (say from 1859 to 1863) of *Once a Week* for sale, secure them: they should be the cherished possessions of every black and white artist. After this date their quality fell off. Charles Keene contributed to *Once a Week* some of his best work, and the Mr. Millais of that date in line is more interesting than the Sir John Millais of to-day in paint. There is, in especial, a beautiful drawing by him, an illustration to the *Grandmother's Apology*, in the volume for 1859, page 40. But, frankly, it is a mistake to instance one illustration where so very many are monumental productions. Fred Walker contributed many exquisite drawings; Mr. Whistler, few enough to make us ardently wish there were more; and the same may be said of Mr. Sandys' decorative work—his *Rosamond, Queen of the Lombards*, his *Yet once more let the Organ play*, his *KingW arwulf, Harald Harfagr*, or *The Old Chartist*. These things are a delight: the artist's work so insistently good, the quality of the engraver's lines so wonderfully fine.

For all the talk and pother about illustration, there is nothing to-day that comes within miles of the work done in, say, 1862-1863 for *OnceaW eek*. It would be difficult to over-praise or to over-estimate the value of this fine period. It was the period of the abominable crinoline; but even that hideous fashion was transfigured by the artistry of these men. That is evident in the beautiful drawing, *If*, contributed by Sandys to the *Argosy* for 1863, in which the grandly flowing lines of the dress show what may be done with the most unpromising material.

The most interesting drawings in the *Cornhill Magazine* range from 1863 to 1867. Especially noteworthy are the illustrations by Fred Walker— *Maladetta*, May, 1863, page 621, and *Out of the Valley of the Shadow*, January, 1867, page 75. If you compare the first of these with the little pen-drawing by Charles Green, reproduced by process in *Harper's Magazine*, May, 1891, page 894, entitled, "Give me those letters," you will see how Mr. Green's hand has retained the old technique he and his brother illustrators learnt in drawing for the wood-engraver, and you will observe how well that old handling looks, and how admirably it reproduces in the process-work of to-day. Two other most successful wood blocks from the *Cornhill Magazine* may be noted—*Mother's Guineas*, by Charles Keene, July, 1864, and *Molly'sNewBonnet* , August, 1864, by Mr. Du Maurier.

COMPARATIVE PROCESSES.

Processes, at first chiefly of the heliogravure or photogravure variety—processes, that is to say, of the intaglio or plate-printing description, printed in the same way as etchings and mezzotints, from dots and lines sunken in a metal plate instead of standing out in relief—date back almost to the invention of photography in 1834; and all modern processes of reproducing drawings have a photographic basis. Even at that time it was demonstrated that a glass negative could be used to reproduce the photographic image as an etched plate that would print in the manner of a mezzotint. Mr. H. Fox-Talbot, to whom belongs, equally with Daguerre, the invention of photography, was the first to show this. He devised an etched silver plate that reproduced a photograph direct.

Photo-relief, or type-printing, blocks date from such comparatively recent times as 1860, when the *Photographic Journal* showed an illustration printed from a block by the Pretsch process.

At this present time there are three methods of primary importance for the reproduction of line drawings—

The swelled gelatine process,
The albumen process,
The bitumen process.

The first of these three processes is the most expensive, and it has not so great a vogue as the less costly methods, which are employed for the illustration of journals or publications that do not rely chiefly upon the excellence of their work. It is employed almost exclusively by Messrs. A. and C. Dawson in this country, and it is in all essentials identical with the old Pretsch process that first saw the light thirty-three years ago.

Acids do not enter into the practice of it at all. The procedure is briefly thus: A good dense negative is taken of the drawing to be reproduced to the size required. The glass plate is then placed in perfect contact with gelatine sensitized by an admixture of bichromate of potassium to the action of light.

Placed in water, the gelatine thus printed upon from the negative, swells, excepting those portions that have received the image of the reduced drawing. These are now become sunken, and form a suitable matrix for electrotyping into. Copper is then deposited by electro-deposition. The copper skin receives a backing of type-metal, and is mounted on wood to the height of type, and the block, ready for printing, is completed.

This process gives peculiar advantages in the reproduction of pen-drawings made with greyed or diluted inks. The photographic negative reproduces, of course, the varying intensities of such work with the most absolute accuracy, and they are repeated, with scarcely less fidelity, by the gelatine matrix. Pencil marks and pen-drawings with a slight admixture of pencil come excellently well by this method.

Every pen-draughtsman who sketches from nature knows how, in re-drawing from his pencil sketches, the feeling and sympathy of his work are lost, wholly or in part; but if the finished pen-drawing is made over the original pencil sketch and the pencilling retained, the effect is generally a revelation. It is in these cases that the swelled gelatine process gives the best results.

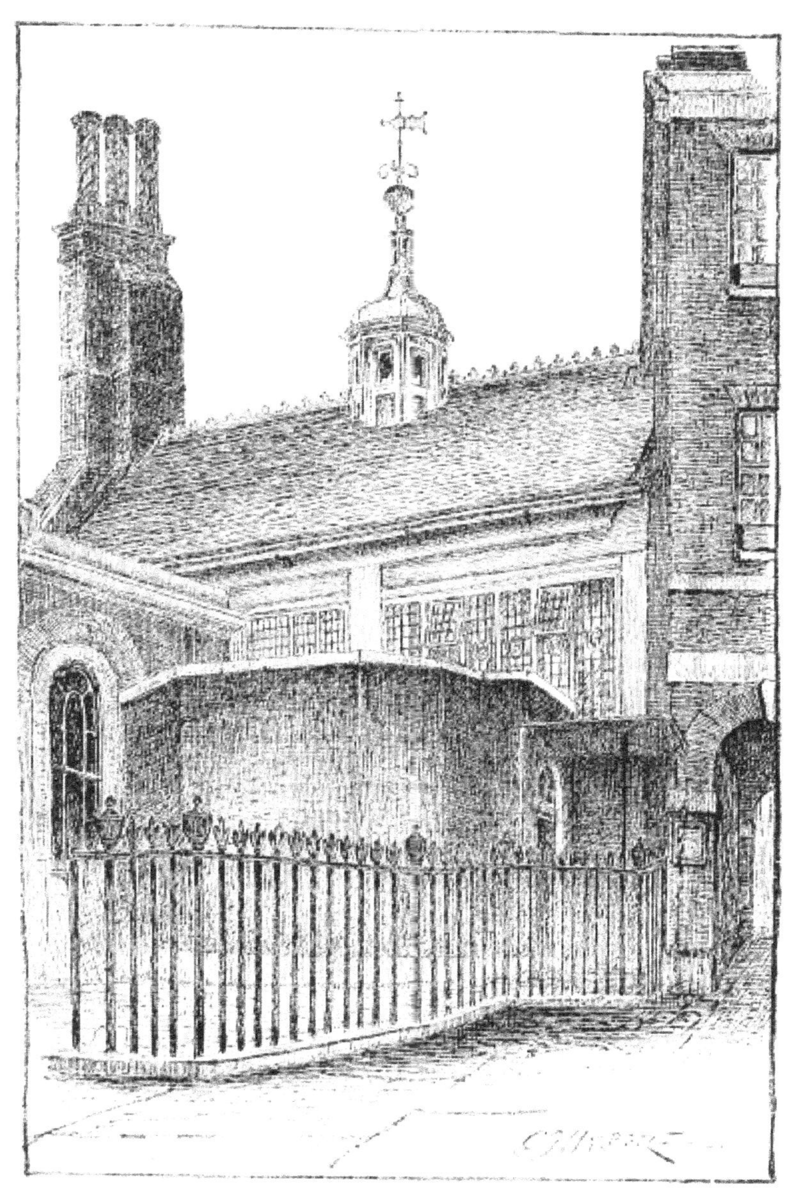

4¾ × 7½.   THE HALL, BARNARD'S INN.

Drawing in pale Indian ink on HP Whatman paper.
Drawn without knowledge of process and reproduced
by the swelled gelatine method.

This example (*The Hall, Barnard's Inn*) of a pen-drawing not made for reproduction by process was made years ago. Now reproduced, it shows that almost everything is possible to mechanical reproduction to-day. This drawing, worked upon with never a thought or idea or knowledge of process, comes every whit as well as if it had been drawn scrupulously to that end. It is all pen-work, save the outline around it and the signature, and they are in black chalk. The reduction from the original is only three-quarters of an inch across, and the reproduction is in every respect exact. Of course it is only swelled gelatine that could perform this feat; but by that process it is clear that you get results at once sympathetic and faithful, without the necessity of caring overmuch about the purely mechanical drudgery of learning a convention in pen and ink that shall be suitable for the etched processes. That convention has been wrought—it may not be said by tears and blood, but certainly with prodigious labour—by the masters of the art of pen-drawing into something artistic and pleasing to the eye, while it satisfies photographic and chemical needs. But here is a process that demands no previous training in drawing for reproduction, and leaves the artist unfettered. True, it opens a vista of easy reproduction to the amateur, which is a thing terrible to think upon; but, on the other hand, to it we owe some delightful reproductions of "painters'" pen-drawings that make the earlier numbers of the illustrated exhibition catalogues worth having.

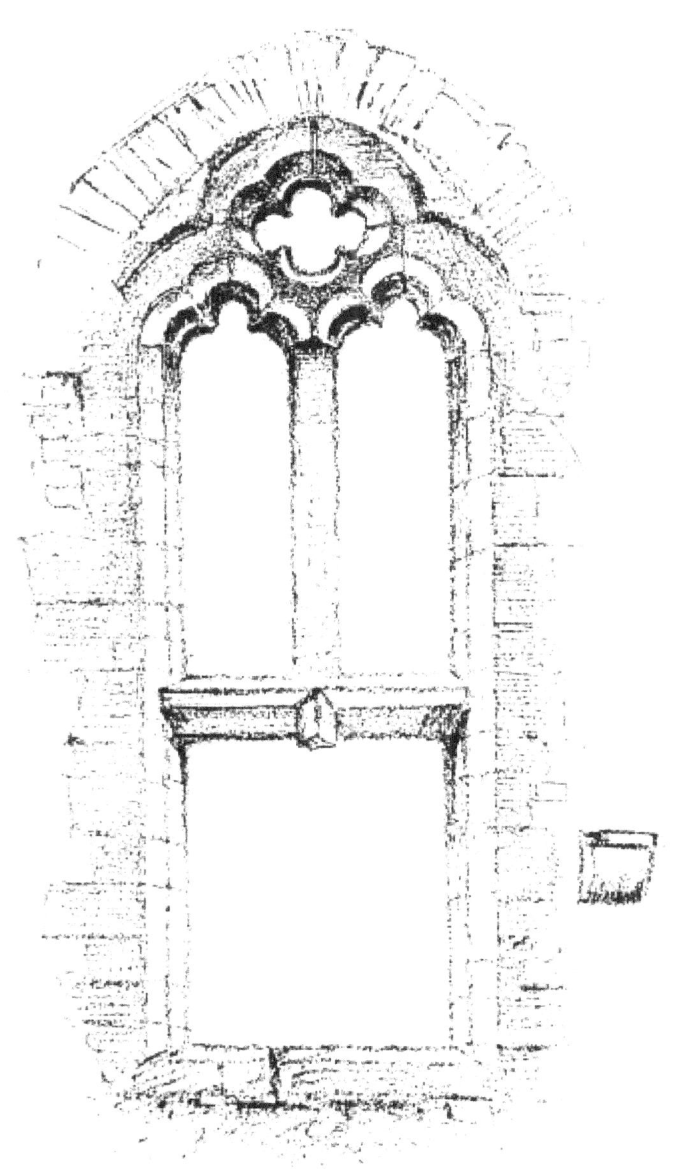

4½ × 8.   A WINDOW, CHEPSTOW CASTLE.

Drawing in Conté crayon on rough paper.

The albumen process is perhaps the more widely used of the three. By it the vast majority of the blocks used in journalistic work are made. It is credibly reported that one firm alone delivers annually sixty-three thousand blocks made by this process, which (it will thus be seen) is particularly suited to reproduction of the most instant and straight-away nature. It is also the cheapest method of reproduction, which goes far toward explaining that gigantic output just quoted. But, on the other hand, the albumen process in the hands of an artist in reproduction (as, for instance, M. Chefdeville) is capable of the most sympathetic results. It gives a softer, more velvety line than one would think possible, a line of a different character entirely from the clear, cold, sharp, and formal line characteristic of processes in which bitumen is used. These two methods (albumen and bitumen) are incapable of reproducing scarcely anything in *fac-simile* but pure line-work; pencil marks or greyed ink are either omitted or exaggerated to extremity, and they can only be corrected by the subsequent use of the graver upon the block. But black chalk or Conté crayon used upon slightly granulated drawing-papers, either by themselves or mixed with pen-work, come readily enough and help greatly to reinforce a sketch. This sketch of *A Window, Chepstow Castle*, was made with a Conté crayon. Unfortunately, these materials smear very easily, and have to be fixed before they can be trusted to the photo-engraver with perfect safety. Drawings made in this way may be fixed with a solution composed of gum mastic and methylated spirits of wine: one part of the former to seven parts of the latter. This fixing solution is best applied with a spray apparatus, as sold by chemists. But better than crayons, chalks, or charcoals are the lithographic chalks now coming somewhat into vogue. They have the one inestimable advantage of fixity, and cannot be readily smeared, even with intent. They are not fit for use upon smooth Bristol-board or glazed paper, but find their best mediums in HP and "not" makes of drawing-paper, and in the grained "scratch-out" cardboards, of which more hereafter. They give greater depth of colour than lead pencil, and reproduce more surely; and the drawings worked up with them readily stand as much reduction as an ordinary pen-drawing. The No. 1 Lemercier is the best variety of lithographic chalks for this admixture; it is harder than others, and can be better sharpened to a fine point. For detail it is to be used very sparingly or not at all, because it is incapable of producing a delicate line; but for giving force, for instance, to a drawing of crumbling walls, or to an impressionist sketch of landscape, it is invaluable. The effects produced by working with a No. 1 Lemercier litho-chalk are shown here. The first example was drawn upon Whatman's "not" paper, which gives a fine, bold granulation. The two remaining examples are from sketches on Allongé paper, a fine-grained charcoal paper of French make.

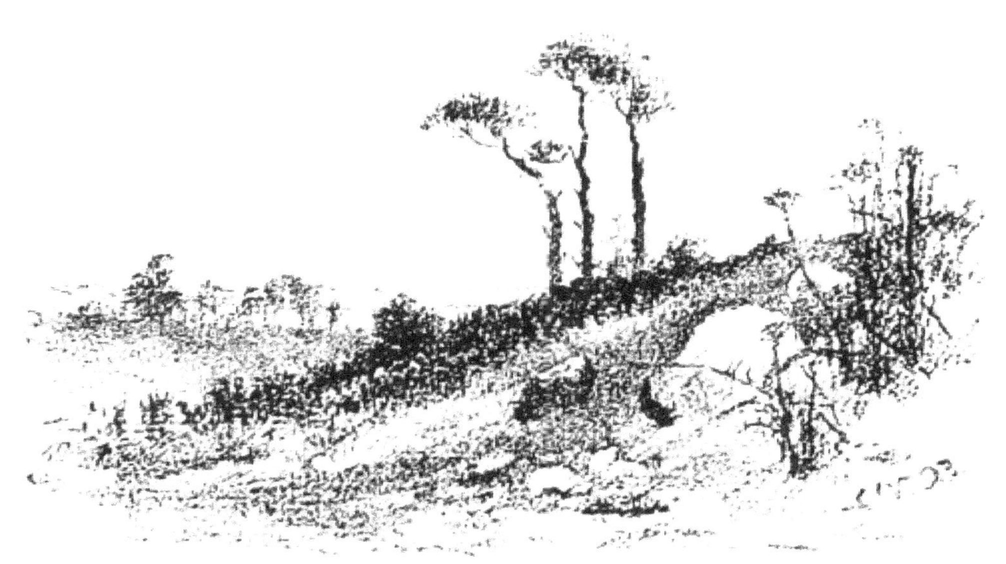

ON WHATMAN'S "NOT" PAPER   (6½ × 4½).

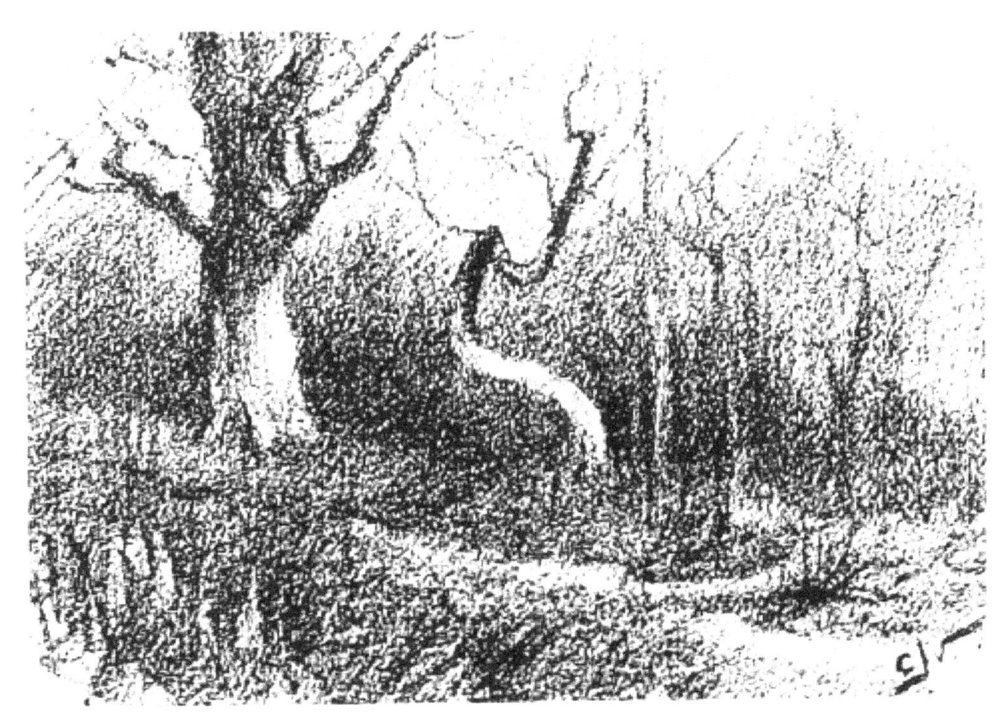

ON ALLONGÉ PAPER, RIGHT SIDE   (6¼ × 4½).

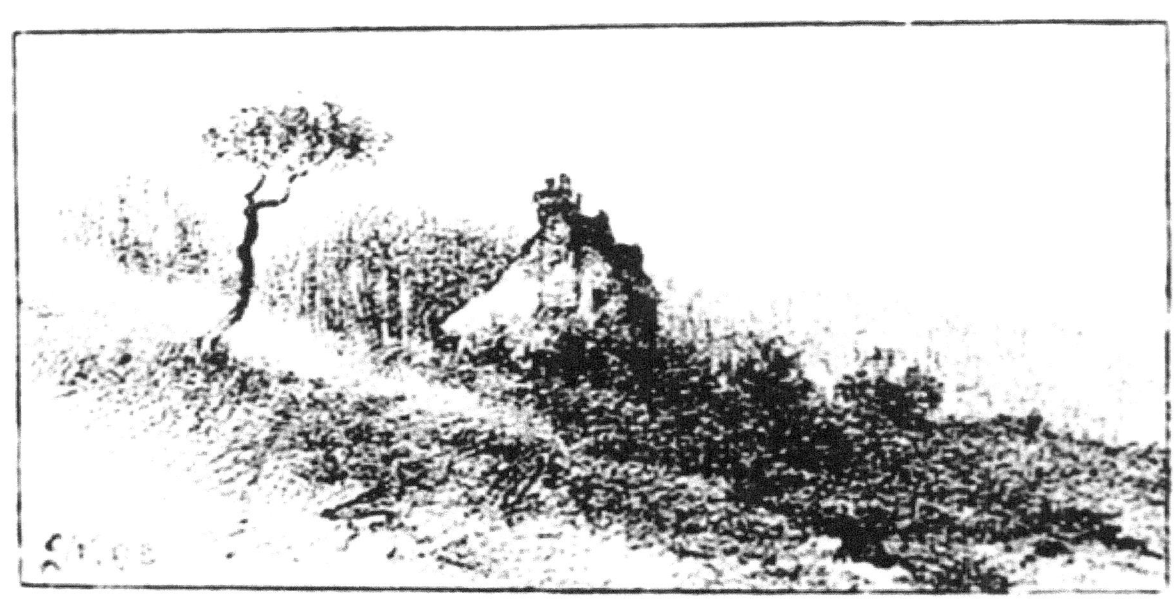

FROM THE DRAWING (4½ × 2½) ON ALLONGÉ PAPER
(RIGHT SIDE).

It is also worth knowing that a good grained drawing may be made with litho-chalk, by taking a piece of dull-surfaced paper, like the kind generally used for type-writing purposes, pinning it tightly upon glass- or sand-paper and then working upon it, keeping it always in contact with the rough sand-paper underneath. A canvas-grain may be obtained by using the cover of a canvas-bound book in the same way.

Both the albumen and the bitumen processes are practised with the aid of acids upon zinc. In the first named the zinc plate is coated with a ground composed of a solution of white of egg and bichromate of ammonia, soluble in cold water. A reversed photographic negative is taken of the drawing and placed in contact with the prepared zinc plate in a specially constructed printing-frame. When the drawing is sufficiently printed upon this albumen surface, the plate is rolled over with a roller charged with printing-ink thinned down with turpentine, and then, when this inking has been completed, the plate is carefully rubbed in cold water until the inked albumen has been rubbed off it, excepting those parts where the drawing appears. The lines composing the drawing remain fixed upon the plate, the peculiar property of the sensitized albumen rendering the lines that have been exposed to the action of light insoluble. The zinc plate is then dried and sponged with gum; dried again, and then the coating of gum washed off, and then inked again. The plate, now thoroughly prepared, is placed in the first etching bath, a rocking vessel filled with much-diluted nitric acid. There are generally three etchings performed upon a zinc block, each successive bath being of progressively stronger acid; and between these baths the plate is gummed, and powdered with resin, and warmed over a gas flame until the printing-ink and the half-melted resin run down the sides of the lines already partly etched; the object of these careful stages being to prevent what is technically termed "under-etching"—that is to say, the production of a relief line, whose section would be thus: ∇ instead of $\wedge$. The result in the printing of an under-etched block would be that the lines would either break or wear down to nothingness, whereas a block showing the second section would grow stronger and the old lines thicker with prolonged use. The section of a wood engraving is according to this second diagram.

In the case of the bitumen process, the photograph is taken as before, the negative placed upon the zinc plate in the same way, and the image printed upon the bitumen. When this has been done, the plate is flooded with turpentine, and all the bitumen dissolved away, with the exception of that upon the image. The subsequent proceedings are as in the case of the albumen process, and need not be recounted.

It will be seen (if this outline can be followed) that the bitumen process differs from the albumen only in the composition of the ground (as an etcher would term it), but the quality of line is very different. The zinc plates used are cut from polished sheets of the metal, from one-sixteenth to one-eighth of an inch in thickness.

A well-etched block should feel sharp yet smooth to the thumb and fingers, as if it were cut. A badly etched or over-etched block has an altogether different feel: scratchy, and repulsive to the touch. Frequently it happens that by carelessness or mischance the process-man will over-etch a block; that is to say, he will allow it to remain in the acid-bath a minute or so too long, so that the upstanding lines become partly eaten away by the fluid. The result, when printed, is a wretched ghost of the original drawing. An over-etched block, or a good block in which the lines appear too thin and the reproduction in consequence weak, can be remedied in degree by being rubbed down with oilstone. This, if the lines are not under-etched, thickens the upstanding metal and produces a heavier print. But some of the smaller process firms have an ingenious, if none too honest, practice of pulling a proof from the *unetched* plate, and sending it along with the defective block. This can readily be done by inking up the image with a roller before printing, and then passing the thin plate of metal through a lithographic press, or through a transfer press, such as is to be found in every process establishment. Of course the print thus secured is a perfect replica in little of the original drawing, and looks eminently satisfactory. One can generally identify these proofs before etching by their backs, which have, of course, not the slightest marks of the pressure usually to be discerned upon even the most carefully prepared proofs of finished blocks. The surface of a zinc block sometimes becomes oxidized by the acid used in etching not having been thoroughly washed off. This may occur at once if the acid is strong, and then it generally happens that the block is irretrievably ruined; but if oxidation occurs after some time, it is generally superficial, and can be rubbed down. The process of oxidation begins with an efflorescence, which may be best rubbed down with a thick stick of charcoal, broken across the grain. But zinc blocks are frequently ruined by carelessness in the printing-office after printing. When the printing has been done it is customary to clean type and blocks from the printing-ink by scrubbing them with a brush dipped in what printers call "lye"—that is, a solution of pearl-ash—which, although it does not injure the leaden types, is apt to corrode the zinc of which most process blocks are made, if they are not carefully and immediately washed in water and dried. A block with its surface destroyed in this manner prints miserably, with a fuzzy appearance. The easiest way of protecting blocks from becoming oxidized is to allow the printing-ink to remain on them, or if you have none, rub them over with tallow.

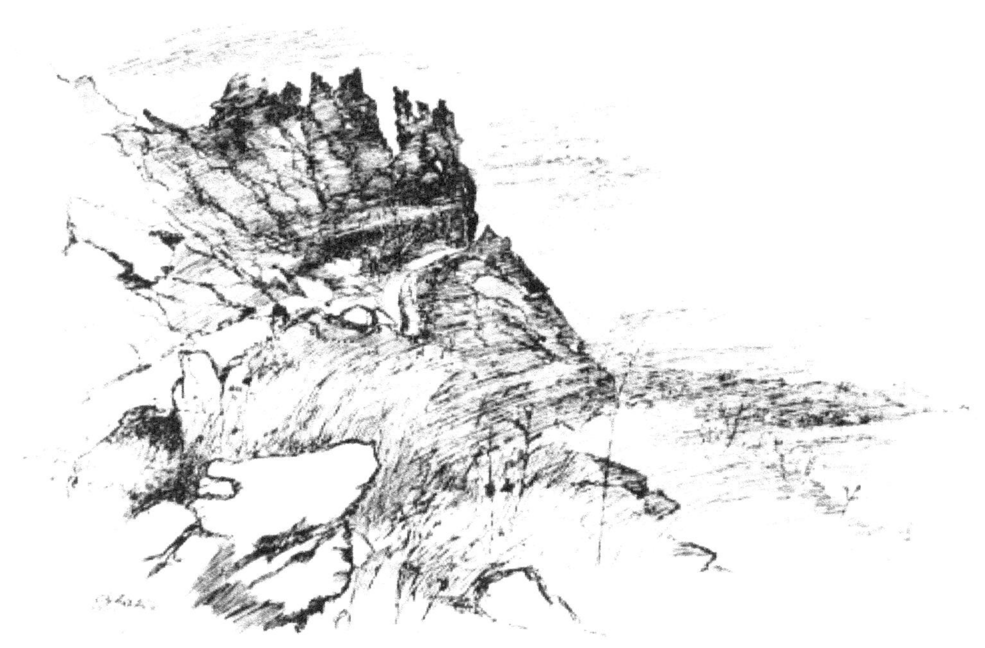

12½ × 9.   BOLT HEAD: A MISTY DAY.

Pen and pencil drawing, reproduced by the bitumen process.

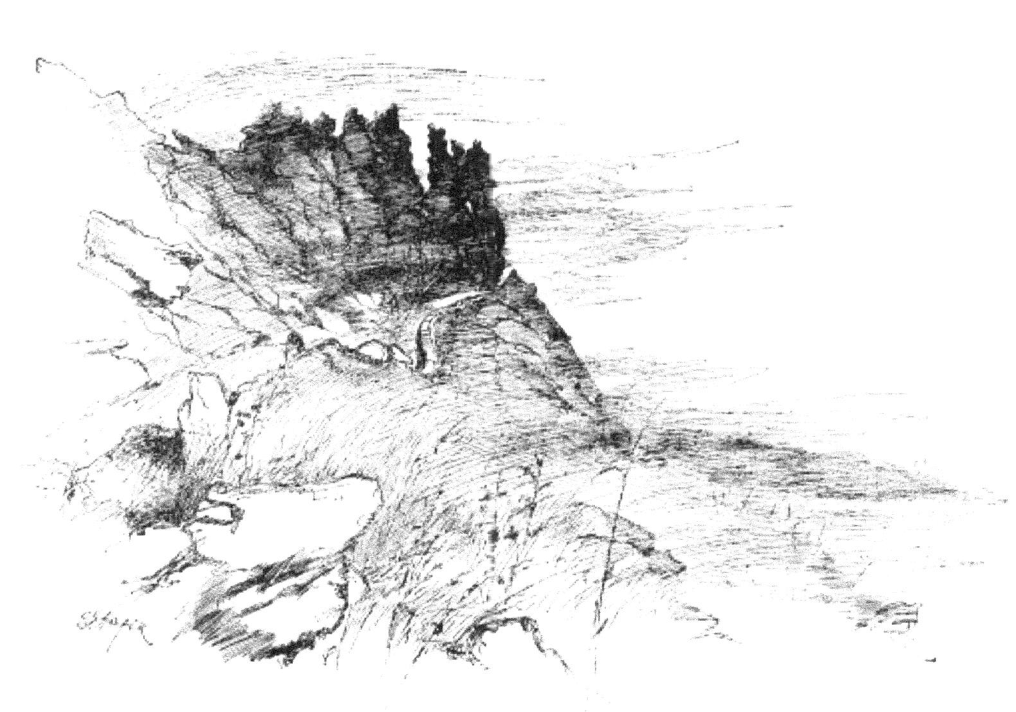

12½ × 9.   BOLT HEAD: A MISTY DAY.

Examples will now be shown of the varying results obtainable from the same drawings by different processes.

The drawing representing a *Misty Day at Bolt Head* was made upon common rough paper, such as is usually found in sailors' log-books; in fact, it was a log-book the present writer used during the greater part of a tour in Devon, nothing else being obtainable in those parts save the cloth-bound, gold-lettered sketch-books whose porterage convicts one at once of amateurishness. And here let me say that a sailor's log-book, though decidedly an unconventional medium for sketching in, seems to be entirely admirable. The paper takes pencil excellently well, and the faint blue parallel lines with which the pages are ruled need bother no one; they will not (being blue) reproduce. To save the freshness of the impression, the sketch was lightly finished in ink, and sent for reproduction uncleaned. The illustration shows the result. It is an example of the bitumen process, whose original sin of exaggerating all the pencil marks which it has been good enough to reproduce at all is partly cloaked by the intervention of hand-work all over the block. You can see how continually the graver has been put through the lines to produce a greyness, yet how unsatisfactory the result!

The drawing was now *sent for reproduction by the swelled gelatine process*. The result is a much more satisfactory block. Everything that the original contained has been reproduced. The sullen blacknesses of the pinnacled rocks are nothing extenuated, as they were in the first example, where they seem comparatively insignificant, and the technical qualities of pen and pencil are retained throughout, and can readily be identified. The same remarks apply even more strongly to the small blocks from the *Note at Gorran*.

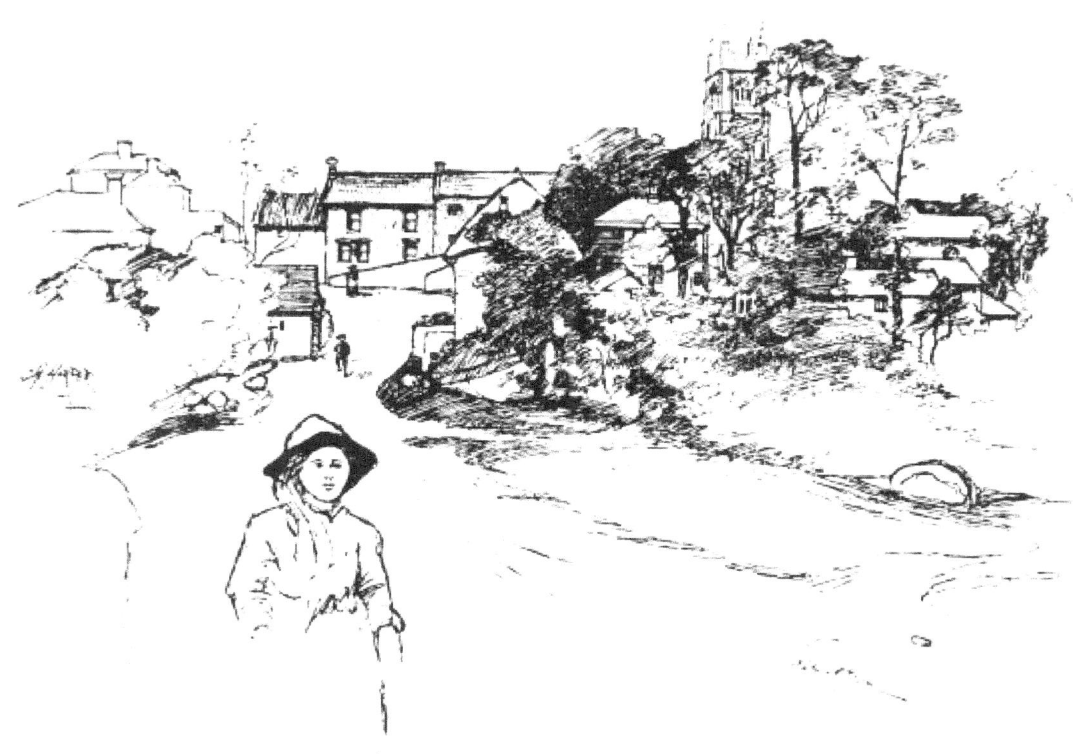

Pen and pencil drawing, reproduced by bitumen process.

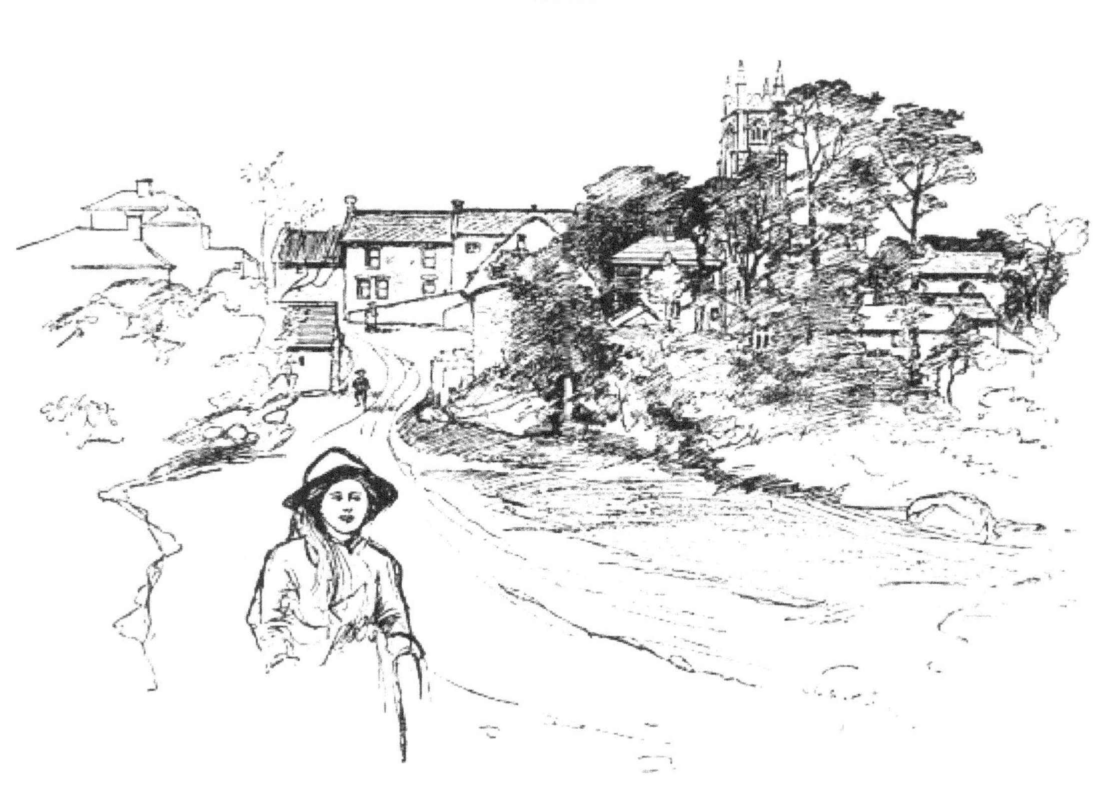

13¼ × 9½.   A NOTE AT GORRAN.

Pen and pencil drawing, reproduced by swelled gelatine process.

But such a pure pen-drawing as that of *Charlwood*, shown here in blocks by (1) Messrs. Dawson's swelled gelatine process, and (2) by Mr. Chefdeville's sympathetic handling of the albumen process, would have come almost equally well by bitumen, or by an ordinary practitioner's treatment of albumen. It offered no technical difficulties, and there is exceedingly little to choose between these two blocks. Careful examination would show that a very slight thickening of line had taken place throughout the block by the gelatine method, and this must ever be the distinguishing difference between that process and those in which acids are used to eat away the metal of the block—that the gelatine renders at its best every jot and tittle of a drawing, and would by the nature of the process rather exaggerate than diminish; and that in those processes in which acids play a part, the process-man must be ever watchful lest his zinc plate be "over-etched"—lest the upstanding metal lines be eaten away to a scratchy travesty of the original drawing. But you will see that although the lines in the swelled gelatine *Charlwood* are appreciably thicker than in its albumen fellow, yet the latter prints darker. The explanation is in the metals of which the two blocks are composed. Zinc prints more heavily than copper.

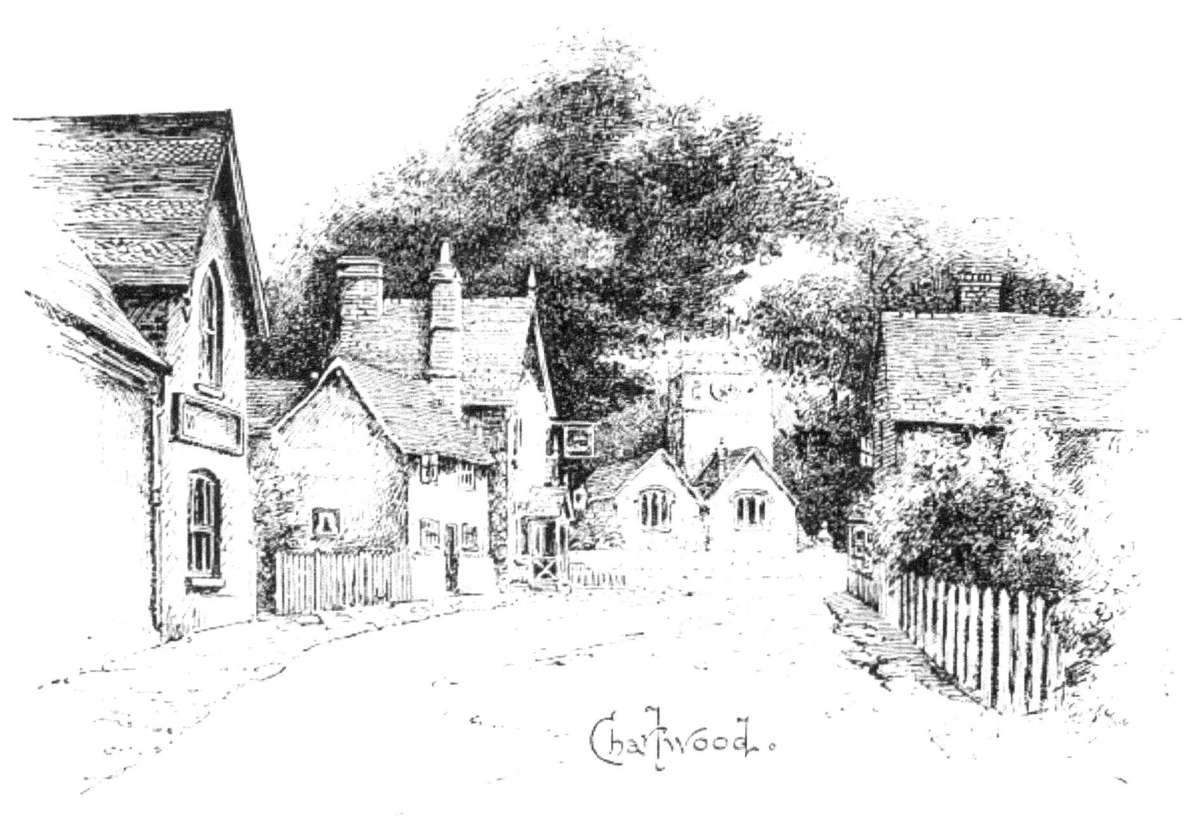

Pen-drawing reproduced by swelled gelatine process.

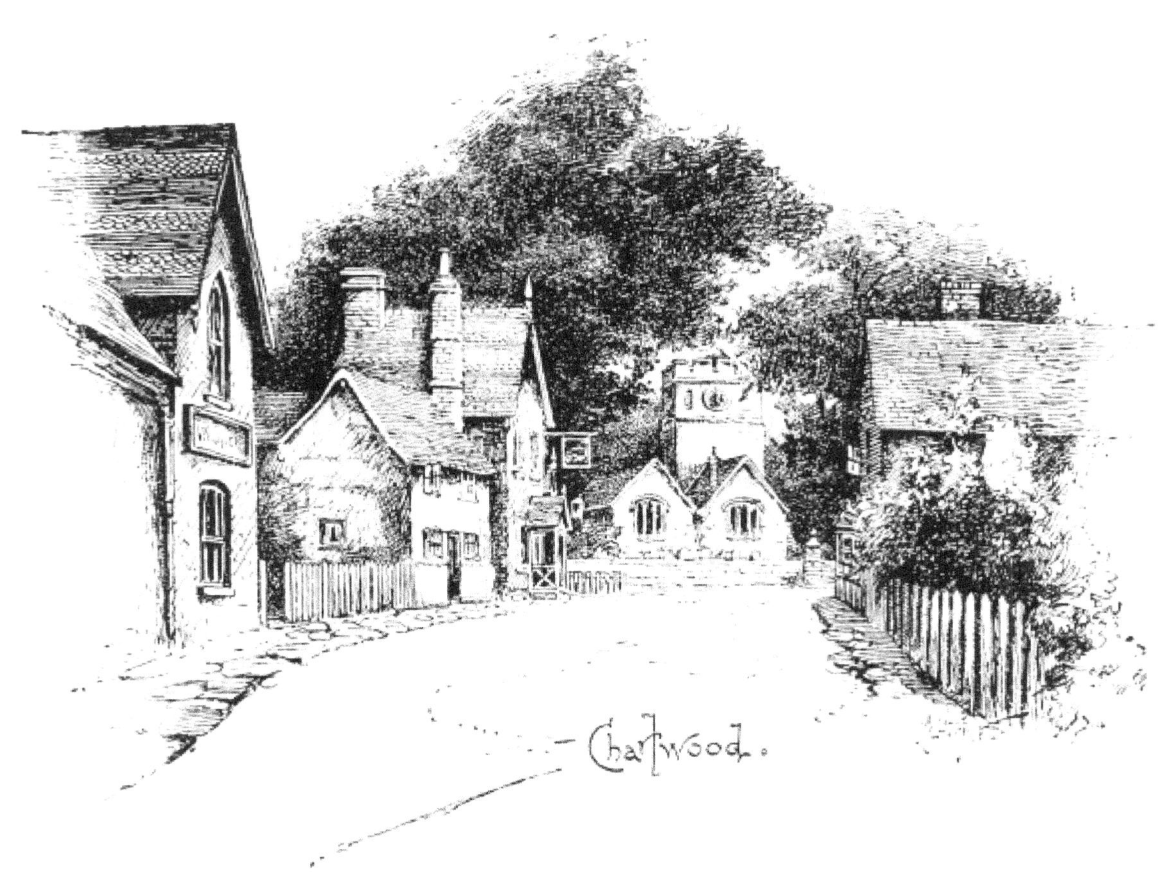

8¼ × 6¼.

Pen-drawing reproduced by Chefdeville.

It should not be forgotten that, to-day, hand-work upon process-blocks is become very usual. To paraphrase a well-worn political catch-phrase, the old methods have been called in to redress the vagaries of the new: the graver has been retained to correct the crudities of the rocking-bath. To be less cryptic, the graver is used nowadays to tone down the harsh and ragged edges of the etched zinc. Here is an illustration that will convey the idea to perfection. Here is, in this *View from the Tower Bridge Works*, a zincographic block, grounded with bitumen and etched by the aid of acids. The original drawing was made upon Bristol-board, with Stephens' ebony stain, and an F nib of Mitchell's make. The size of that drawing was twelve and a half inches across; the sky drawn in with much elaboration. A first proof showed a sky harsh and wanting in aërial perspective. A graver was put through it, cutting up the lines into dots, and thus putting the sky into proper relation with the rest of the picture.

Another interesting and suggestive comparison is between photogravure, or heliogravure, as it is sometimes called, and type-printing processes for the reproduction of line. The frontispiece to this volume is a heliogravure plate by Dujardin, of Paris, from a pen-drawing that offered no obstacles to adequate reproduction by the bitumen process. In fact, you see it here, reproduced in that way, and of the same size. The copper intaglio plate is in every way superior to the relief block, as might have been expected. The hardness of the latter method gives way, in the heliogravure plate, to a delightful softness, even when the plate is clean-wiped and printed in as bald and artless a fashion as a tradesman's business card; but now it is printed with care and with the *retroussage* that is generally the meed of the etching, you could not have distinguished it *from* an etching had you not been told its history.

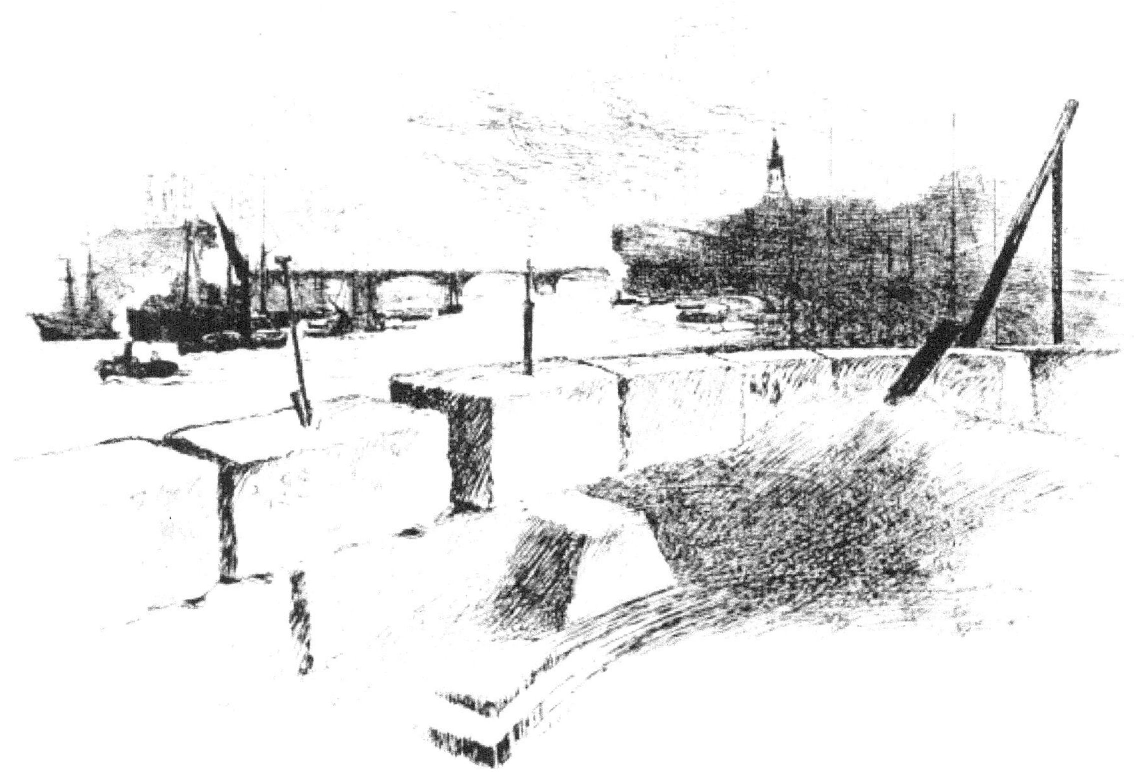

12½ × 9.　　　VIEW FROM THE TOWER BRIDGE WORKS.

Bitumen process.

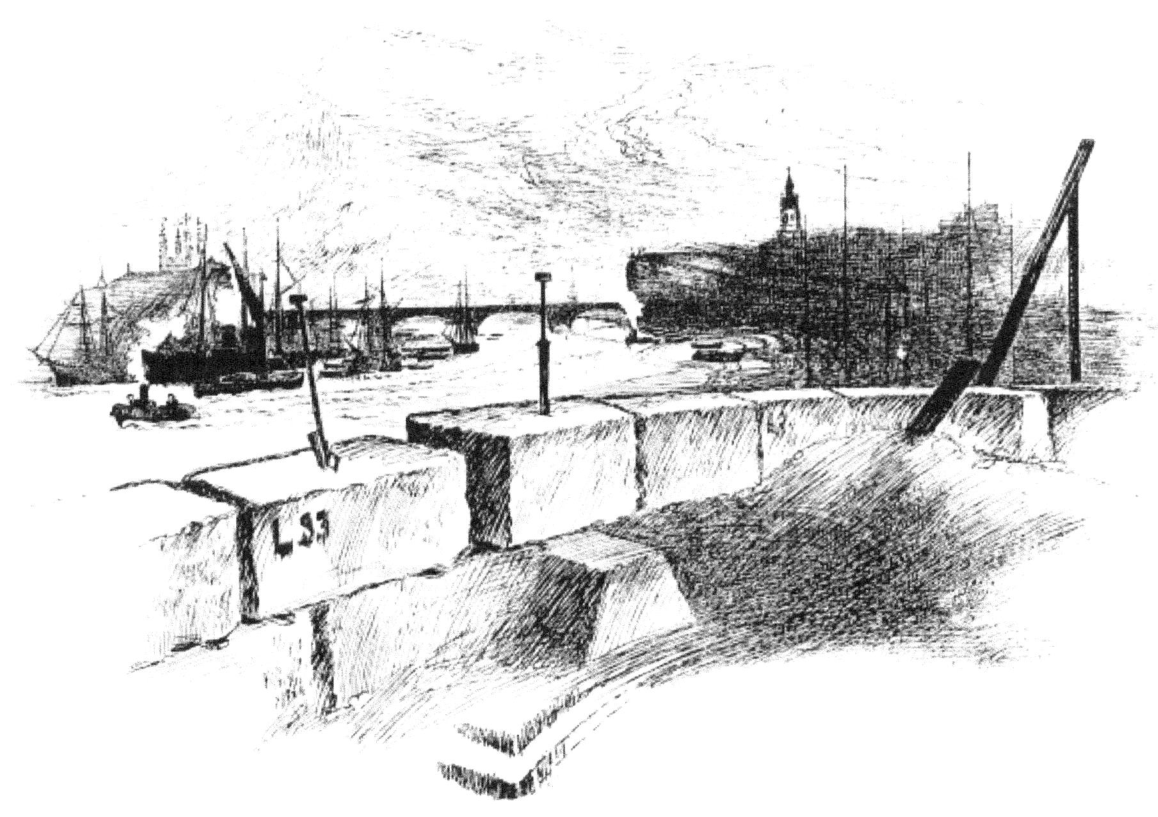

12½ × 9.   VIEW FROM THE TOWER BRIDGE WORKS.

Bitumen process. Sky revised by hand-work.

The procedure in making a heliogravure is in this wise:—A copper plate, similar to the kind used by etchers, receives a ground of bichromatized bitumen. A photograph is taken of the drawing to be reproduced, and from the negative thus obtained a *positive* is made. The positive, in reverse, is placed upon the grounded plate and printed upon it. The bitumen which has been printed upon by the action of light is thus rendered wholly insoluble, and the image of the drawing remains the only soluble portion of the ground. The plate is then treated with turpentine, and the soluble lines thus dissolved. Follows then the ordinary etching procedure. This is a more simple and ready process than the making of a relief block. It is, however, more expensive to commission, but then expense never is any criterion of original cost. The printing, though, is a heavy item, because, equally with etchings or mezzotints, it must be printed upon a copper-plate press, and this involves the cleaning and the re-inking of the plate with every impression.

The subject which the present plate bears does not show the utmost capabilities of the heliogravure. It was chosen as a fair example to show the difference between two methods without straining the limitations of the relief block. But if the drawing had been most carefully graduated in intensity from the deepest black to the palest brown, the copper plate would have shown everything with perfect ease. Large editions of these plates are not to be printed without injury, because the constant wiping of the soft copper wears down the surface. But to obviate this defect a process of *acierage* has been invented, by which a coating of iron is electrically deposited upon the surface of the plate, rendering it, practically, as durable as a steel engraving.

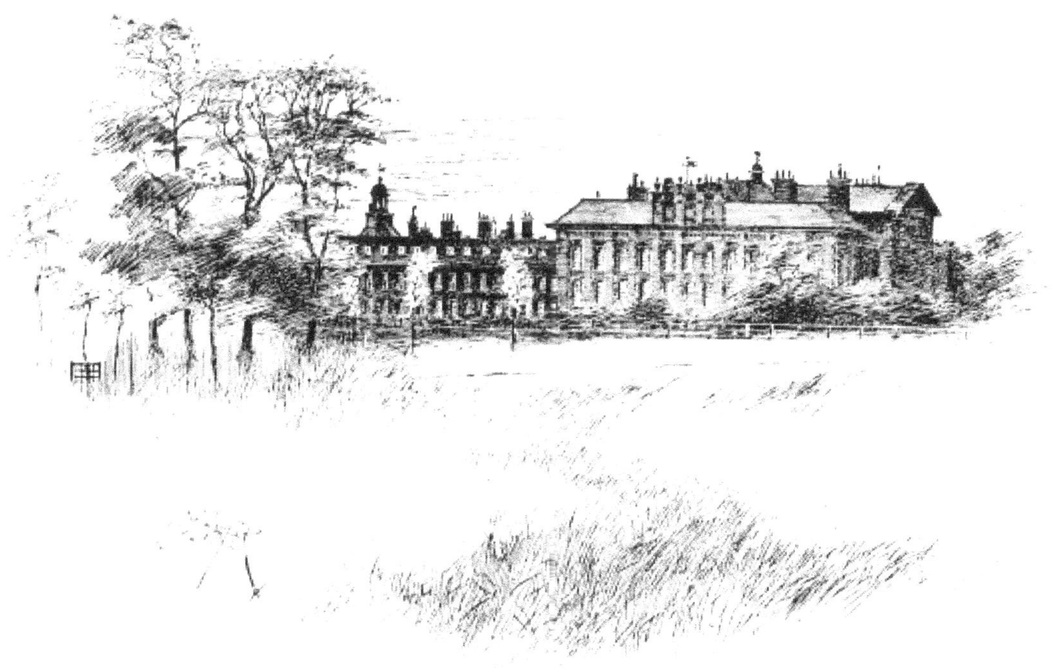

11½ × 7½.   KENSINGTON PALACE.

Bitumen process.

It is by experiments we learn to achieve distinction; by immediate failure that we rise to ultimate success; and ofttimes by pure chance that we discover in these days some new trick of method by which process shall do for the illustrator something it has not done before. There is still, no doubt, in the memory of many, that musty anecdote of the painter who, fumbling over the proper rendering of foam, applied by some accident a sponge to the

wet paint, and lo! there, by happy chance, was the foam which had before
been like nothing so much as wool.

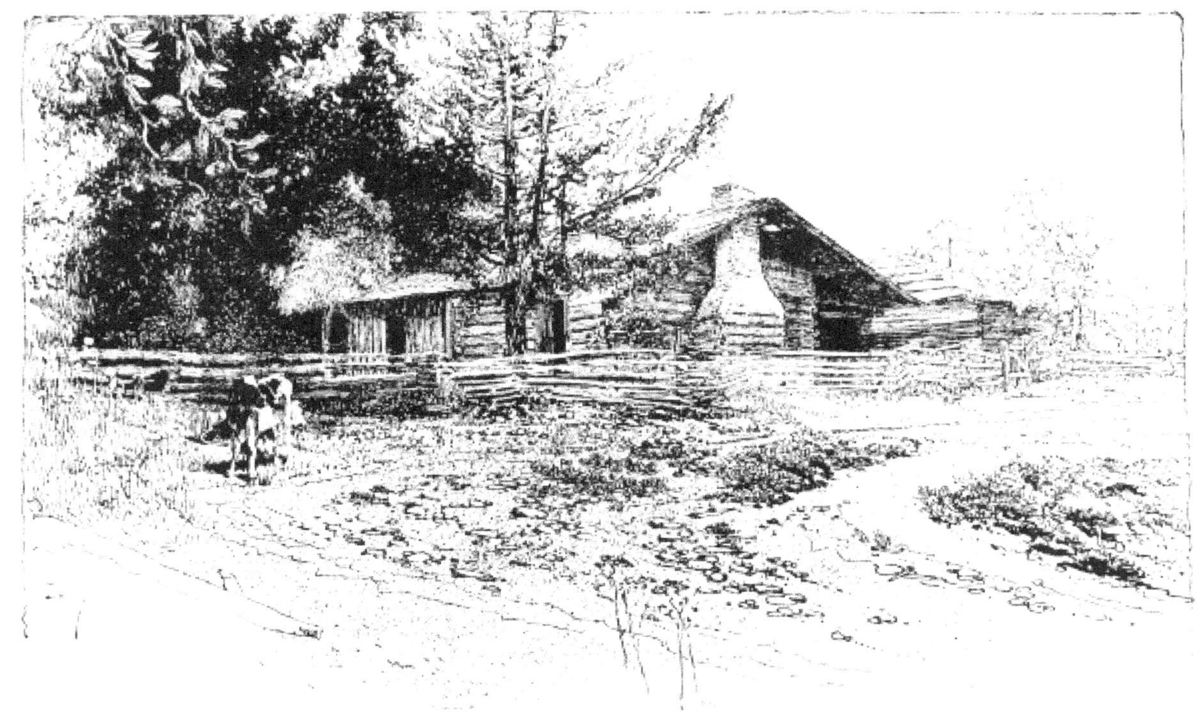

SNODGRASS FARM.

From a drawing by Harry Fenn. An example of splatter-work.

In the same way, I suppose, some draughtsman discovered splatter-
work. He may readily be imagined, prior to this lucky chance, painfully
stippling little dots with his pen; pin-points of ink stilted and formal in
effect when compared with the peculiarly informal concourse of spots
produced by taking a small, stiff-bristled brush (say a toothbrush), inking it,
and then, holding the bristles downwards and inclining toward the drawing,
more or less vigorously stroking the inky bristles *towards* one with a match-
stick. Holding the brush thus, and stroking it in this way, the bristles send a
shower of ink spots upon the drawing. Of course this trick requires an
extended practice before it can be performed in workmanlike fashion, and
even then the parts not required to be splattered have to be carefully
covered with cut-paper masks. [*Mem.*—To use a fixed ink for drawings on
which you intend to splatter, because it is extremely probable that you will
require to paint some portions out with Chinese white, and Chinese white
upon any inks that are not fixed is the despair of the draughtsman.] Here is

an _excellent example of splatter_. It is by that resourceful American draughtsman, Harry Fenn. Indeed, the greatest exponents of this method are Americans: few men in this country have rendered it with any frequency, or with much advantage. I have essayed its use to aid this sunset view of _Black Rock_, and to me it seems to come well. But the finer spots are very difficult of reproduction; some are lost here. There is a most ingenious contrivance, an American notion, I believe, for the better application of splatter. It is called the air-brush, and it consists of a tube filled with ink, and fitted with a description of nozzle through which the ink is projected on to paper by a pneumatic arrangement worked by the artist by means of a treadle. You aim the affair at your drawing, work your treadle, and the trick is done. The splatter is remarkably fine and equable, and its intensity can be regulated by the distance at which the nozzle is held from the drawing. The greater advantage, however, in the use of the air-brush would seem to lie with the lithographic draughtsmen, who have to cover immense areas of work.

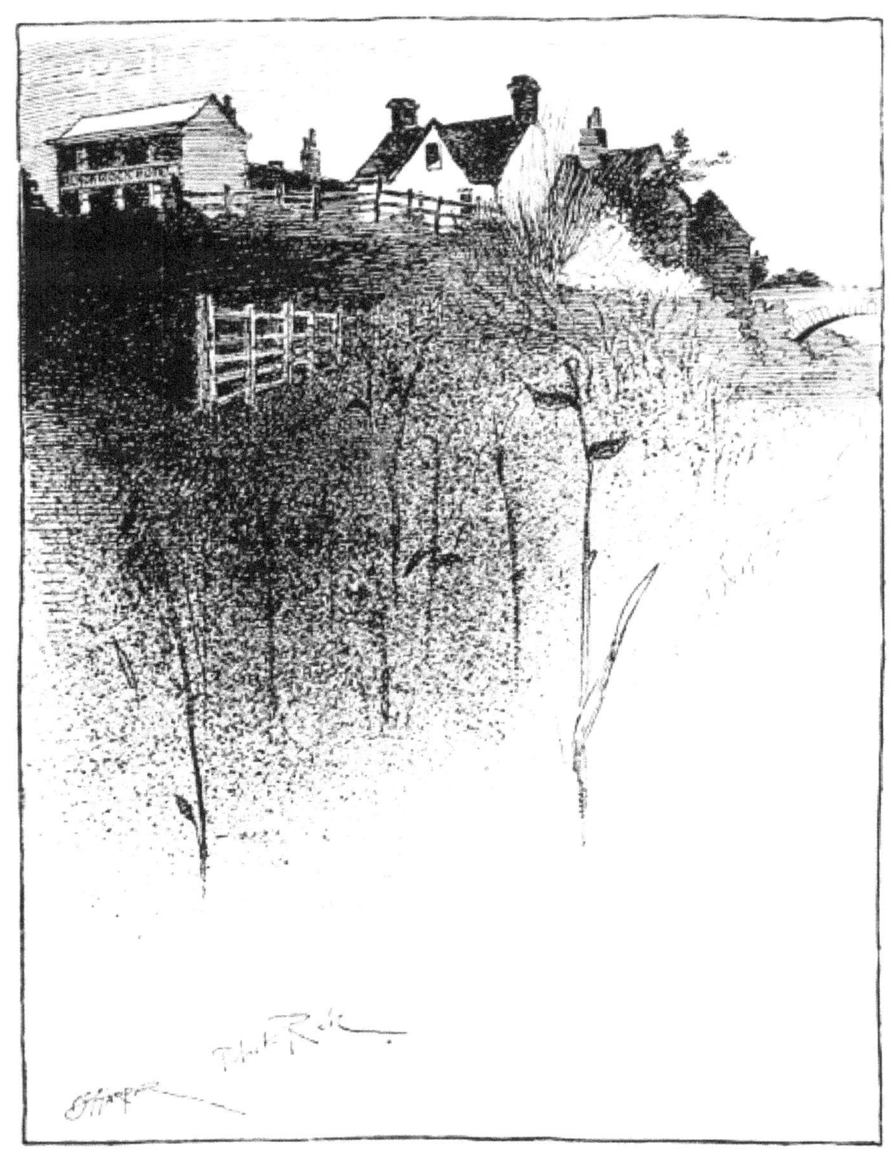

6 × 8¼.   SUNSET, BLACK ROCK.

Splatter-work.

Here follows <u>an experiment with diluted inks</u>: the drawing made upon
HP Whatman with all manner of nibs. It is all pen-work, worked with black
stain, and with writing ink watered down to different values. This is an
attempt to render as truthfully as possible (and as unconventionally) the
sunset shine and shadow of a lonely shore, blown upon with the wild winds
of the Channel. A little stream, overgrown with bents and waving rushes,
flows between a break in the low cliffs and loses itself in the sands. The sun
sets behind the ruined house, and between it and the foreground is a clump

of storm-bent trees, constrained to their uneasy inward pose not by present breezes, but to this shrinking habit of growth by long-continued stress of weather. The block is by Gillot, of Paris, who was asked to get the appearance of the original drawing in a line-block. This he has not altogether succeeded in doing: perhaps it was impossible; but the *feeling* is here. It is a line-block, rouletted all over in the attempt to get the effect produced by watered inks. The roulettes, by which these greynesses are produced, are peculiar instruments, consisting of infinitesimal wheels of hard steel whose edges are fashioned into microscopically small points or facets. Mounted at the end of a stick more nearly resembling a penholder than anything else, the wheel is driven along (and into) the surface of the metal by pressure, making small indentations in it. There are varieties of roulettes, the differences between them lying in the patterns of the projections from the wheel. The varieties in the texture of rouletting seen in this print are thus explained.

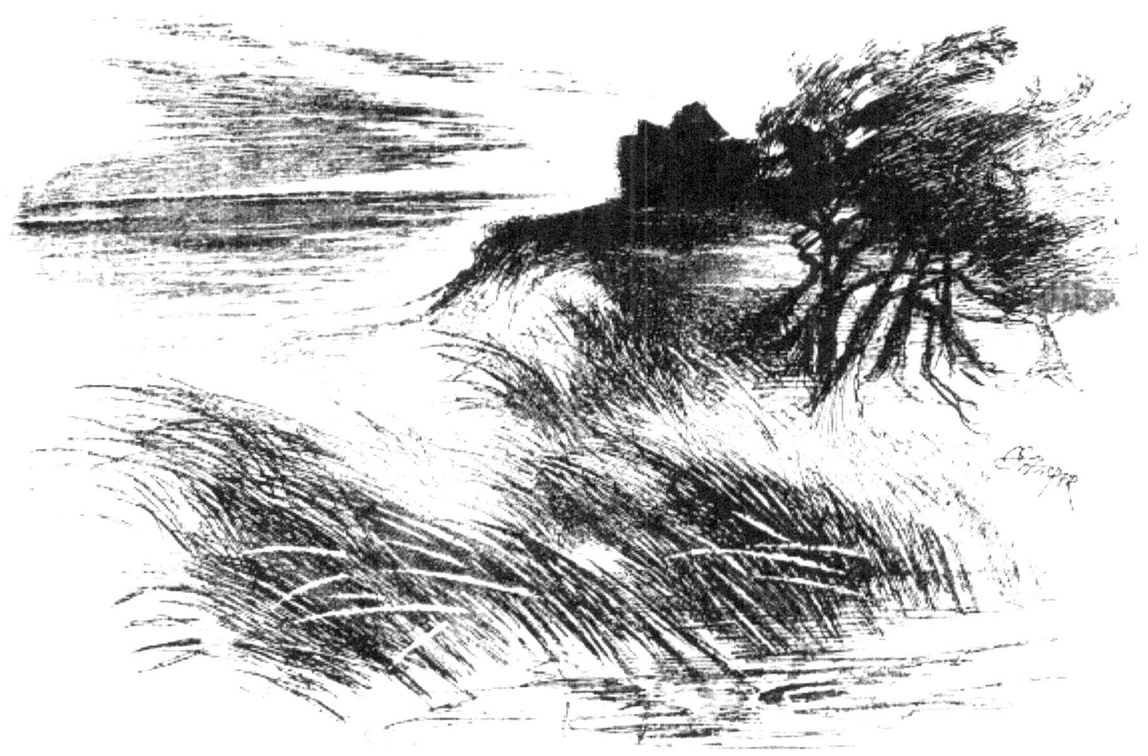

10 × 6½.   DRAWING IN DILUTED INKS, REPRODUCED BY
GILLOT.

Block touched up by hand and freely rouletted.

Now come some experiments in mixtures. The mixed drawing has many possibilities of artistic expression, and here are some essays in mixtures, harnessed to tentative employments of process.

First is this experiment in pen and pencil reproduced in half-tone. It is a view of _Chepstow Castle_—that really picturesque old border fortress—from across the river Wye, a river that comes rushing down from the uplands with an impetuous current full of swirls and eddies. The town of Chepstow lies at the back, represented in this drawing only by its lights. The huts and sheds that straggle down to the waterside, and the rotting pier, where small vessels load and unload insignificant cargoes, are commonplace enough, but they go to make a fine composition; and the last sunburst in the evening sky, the stars already brilliant, and the white gleams from the hurrying river, are immensely valuable, and things of joy to the practitioner in black and white. Rain had fallen during the day, and, when the present writer sat down to sketch, still lent a fine impending juicy air to the scene that seemed incapable of adequate translation into pure line; therefore, upon the pencil sketch was added pen-work, and to that more pencil, and, when finished, the drawing was sent to be processed, with special instructions that the white spaces in the sky should be preserved, together with those on the buildings, but that all else might acquire the light grey tint which the half-tone always gives, as of a drawing made upon paper of a silvery grey. In the result you can see this purely arbitrary, but delightful, ground tint everywhere; it gives absolutely the appearance of a drawing made upon tinted cardboard, but, truly, the only paper employed was a common, rough make, that would be despised of the lordly amateur. Here you see the half-tone process on its best behaviour, and I think it has secured a very notable result.

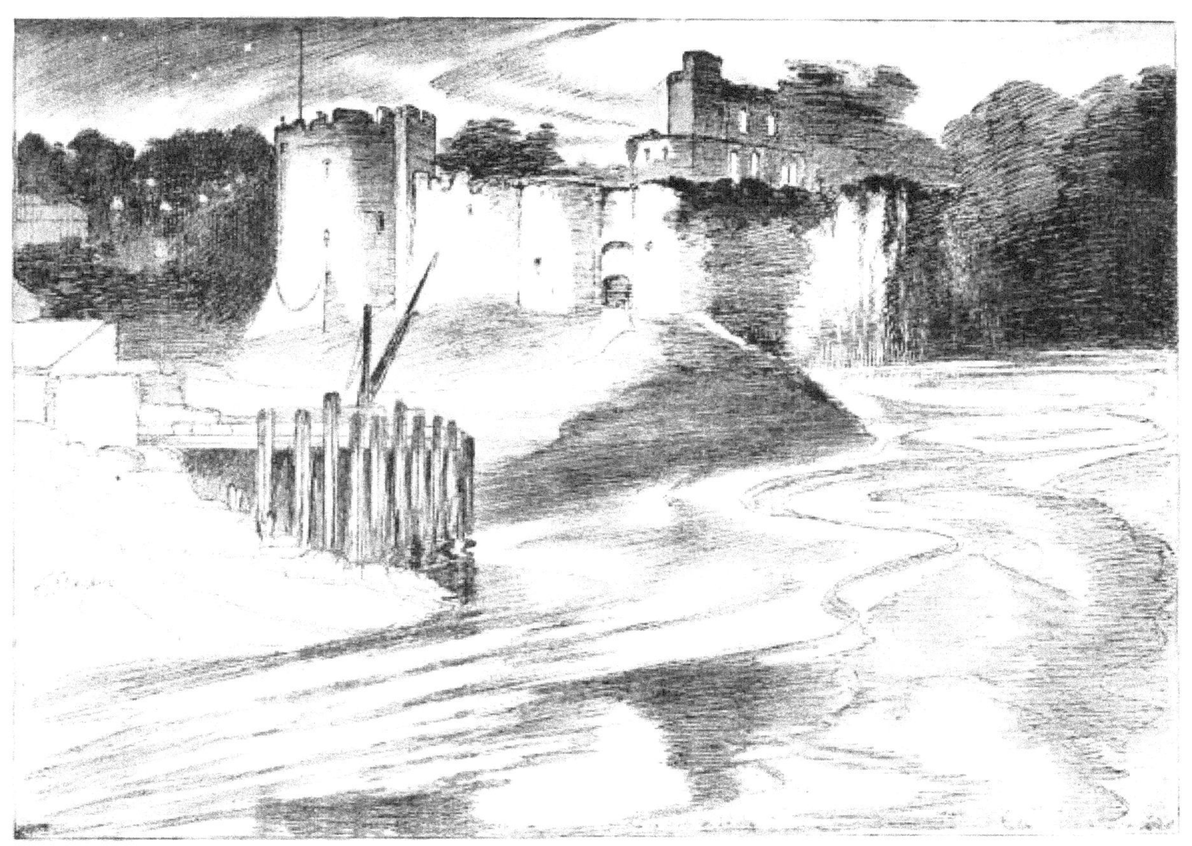

11¾ × 8¾.   CHEPSTOW CASTLE.

Drawing in pen and ink and pencil made on rough paper.
Reproduced by half-tone process.

Here is another experiment, *Clifford's Inn: a Foggy Night*—a mixture of pen and ink and crayon worked upon with a stump, and then lightly brushed over with a damp, not a full, brush; the lights in the windows and the reflections taken out with the point of an eraser.

It should be said that in drawing thus for half-tone reproduction the drawing should be made much more emphatic than the print is intended to appear; that is to say, the deepest shadows should be given an additional depth, and the fainter shading should be a shade lighter than you would give to a drawing not made with a view to publication. If these points are not borne in mind, the result is apt to be flat and featureless.

If a half-tone block exhibits these disagreeable peculiarities, high lights can always be created by the aid of a chisel used upon the metal surface of the block. The more important process firms generally employ a staff of competent engravers, who, now that wood engraving is less widely used, have turned their attention to just this kind of work—the correcting of process-blocks. The artist has but to mark his proof with the corrections and alterations he requires. The two illustrations shown on page 68, from different states of the same block, give a notion of correcting the flatness of half-tone. The second block shows a good deal of retouching in the lights taken out upon the paper and the jug, and in the hatching upon the drinking-horn.

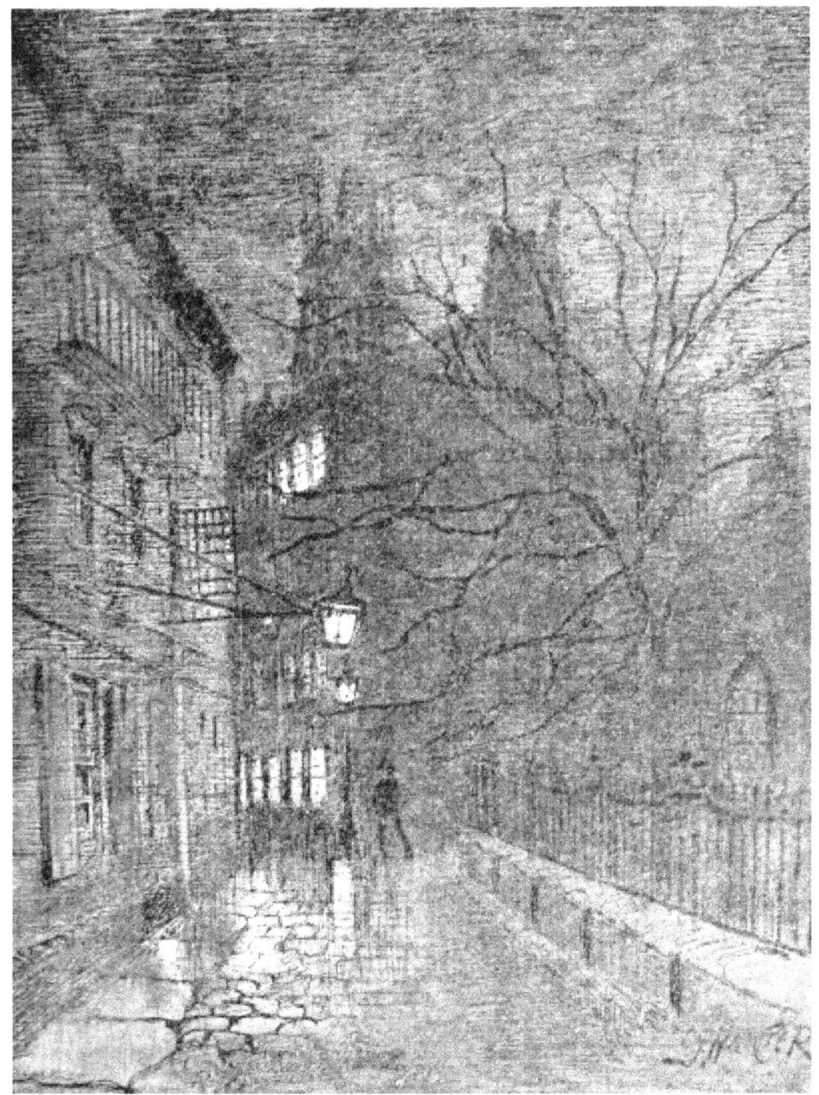

9½ × 6¾.   CLIFFORD'S INN: A FOGGY NIGHT.

Drawn in pen and ink and crayon, and brushed over.
Reproduced by half-tone process, medium grain.

<u>Half-tone processes</u> are practised in much the same way as the albumen and bitumen line methods already described, in so far as that they are worked with acids and upon zinc or copper. At first these half-tone blocks were made in zinc, but recently some reproductive firms have preferred to use copper. Messrs. Waterlow and Sons, in this country, generally employ copper for half-tone blocks from drawings or photographs. Copper prints a softer and more sympathetic line, and does not accumulate dirt so readily as zinc. All the half-tone blocks in this volume are in copper. By these processes the photographs that one sees reproduced direct from nature appear in print without the aid of the artist. They are often referred to as the Meisenbach process, because the Meisenbach Company was amongst the first to use these methods in this country. The essential difference in their working is that there is a ruled screen of glass interposed between the drawing or object to be photographed and the negative. Generally a screen of glass is closely ruled with lines crossing at right angles, and etched with hydrofluoric acid. Into the grooves thus produced, printing-ink is rubbed. The result is a close network of black lines upon glass. This screen, interposed between the sensitized plate in the camera and the object to be photographed, produces upon the negative the criss-cross appearance we see in the ultimate picture. In the half-tone reproductions by Angerer and Göschl, of Vienna, this appearance is singularly varied. The screen used by them is said to be made from white silk of the gauziest description, hung before a wall covered with black velvet in such a manner that the blackness of the velvet can be seen and photographed through the silken film. A negative is made, and from it a positive is produced, which exhibits a curiously varied arrangement of dots and meshes. The positive is used in the same way as the ruled-glass screens.

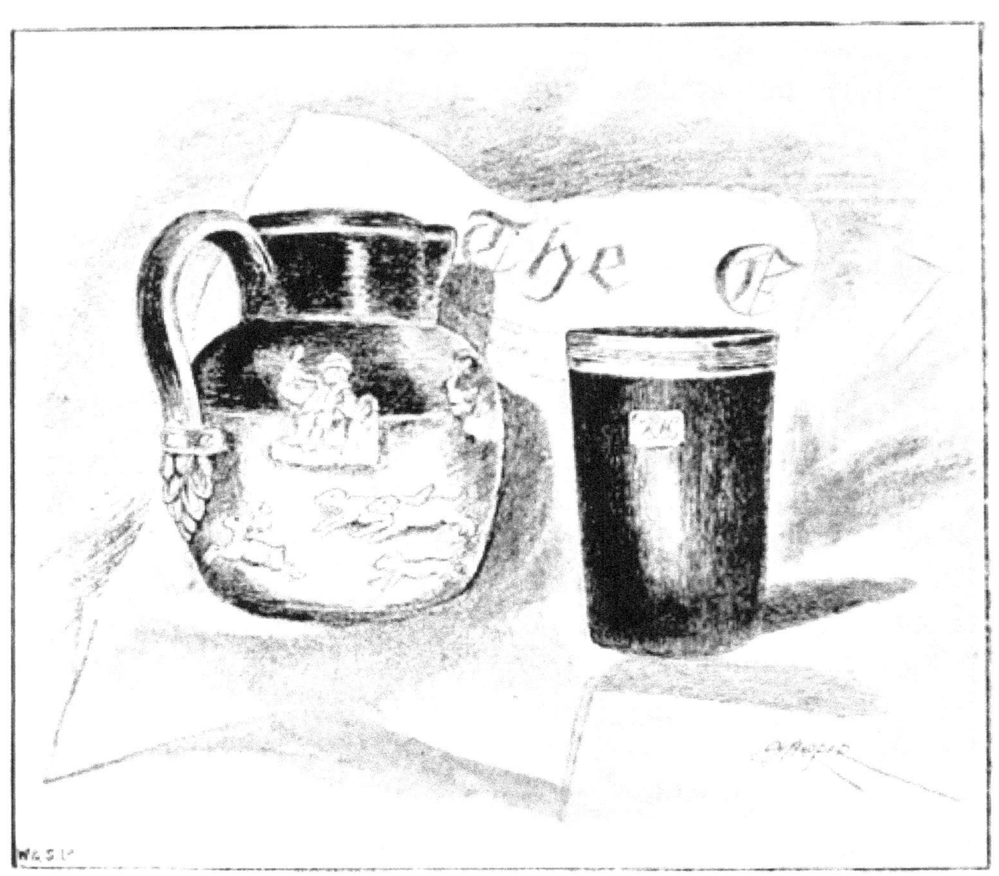
The T

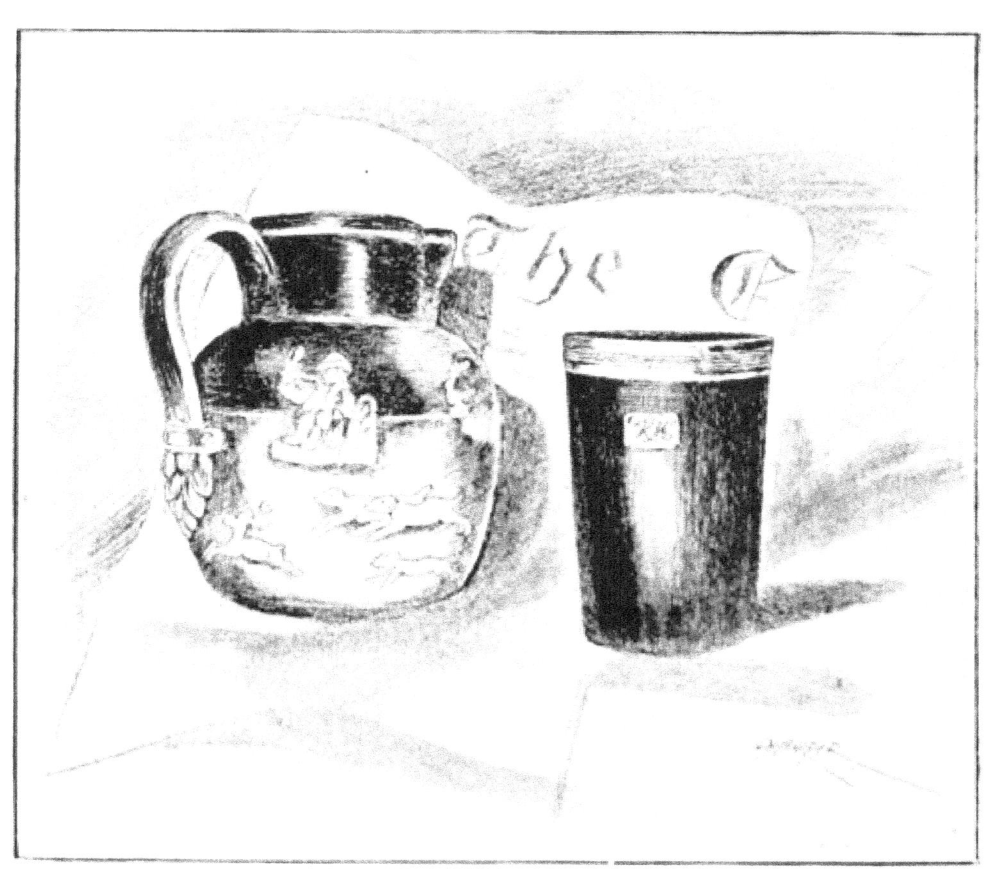

6¾ × 6¼.   PENCIL AND PEN AND INK DRAWING REPRODUCED
BY HALF-TONE PROCESS.

The network characteristic of half-tone relief blocks can be made fine, or medium, or coarse, as required. The fine-grained blocks are used for careful book and magazine printing, and the medium-grained for printing in the better illustrated weeklies; the coarse-grained are used for rougher printing, but still are nearly always too fine for newspaper work. The *Daily Graphic*, however, has solved the problem of printing them sufficiently well for the picture to be discerned. Beyond this the rotary steam-printing press has not yet advanced.

In appearance somewhat similar to a half-tone block, but with the tint differently applied, is the illustration of *The Village Street, Tintern: Night*. Here is a pure pen-drawing, scratched and scribbled to blackness without much care for finesse, the great reduction and the tint being reckoned upon to assuage all angularities. The original drawing was then lightly scribbled over with blue pencil to indicate to the process-man that a mechanical tint was required to be applied upon the block, and word was specially sent that the tint was to be squarely cut, not vignetted. The result seems happy. This is a line block, not tone.

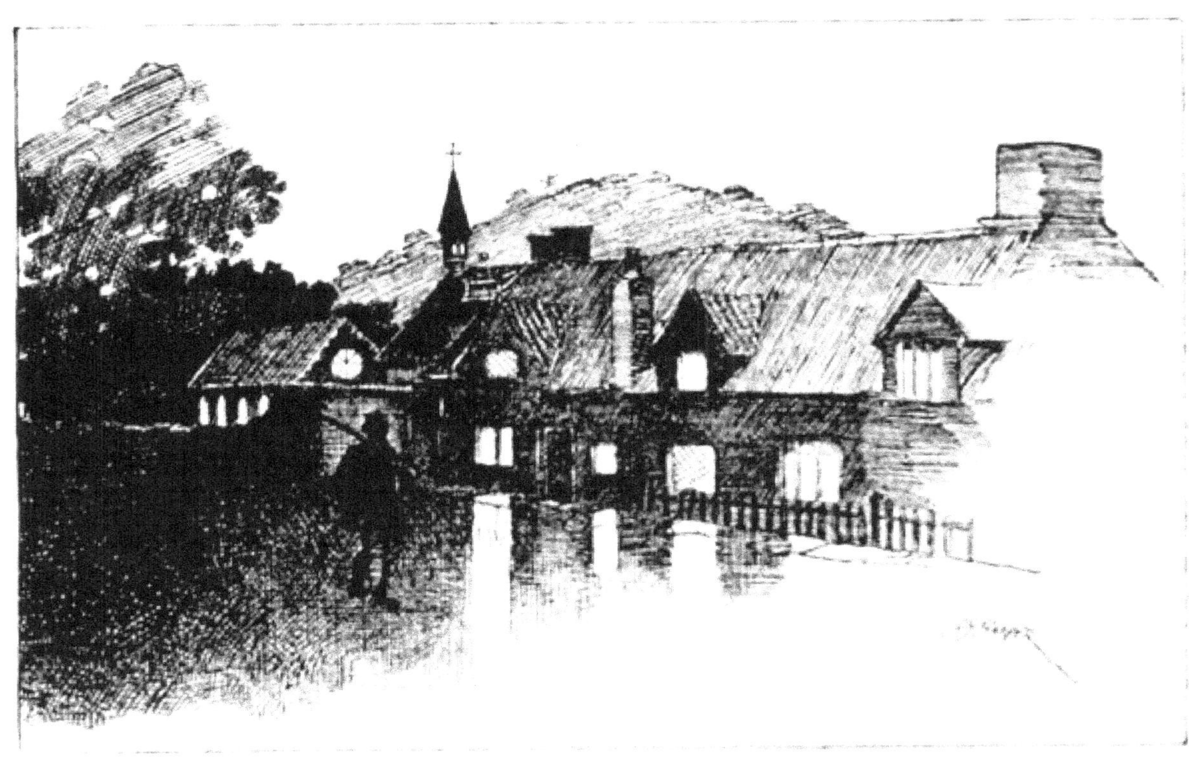

11½ × 9.   THE VILLAGE STREET, TINTERN. NIGHT.

Application of shading medium.

In such a case the procedure is normal until the image is printed upon the sensitized ground of the zinc plate. Then the prescribed tint is transferred by pressure of thumb and fingers, or by means of a burnisher, from an engraved sheet of gelatine previously inked with a printing roller. The zinc plate is then etched in the familiar way.

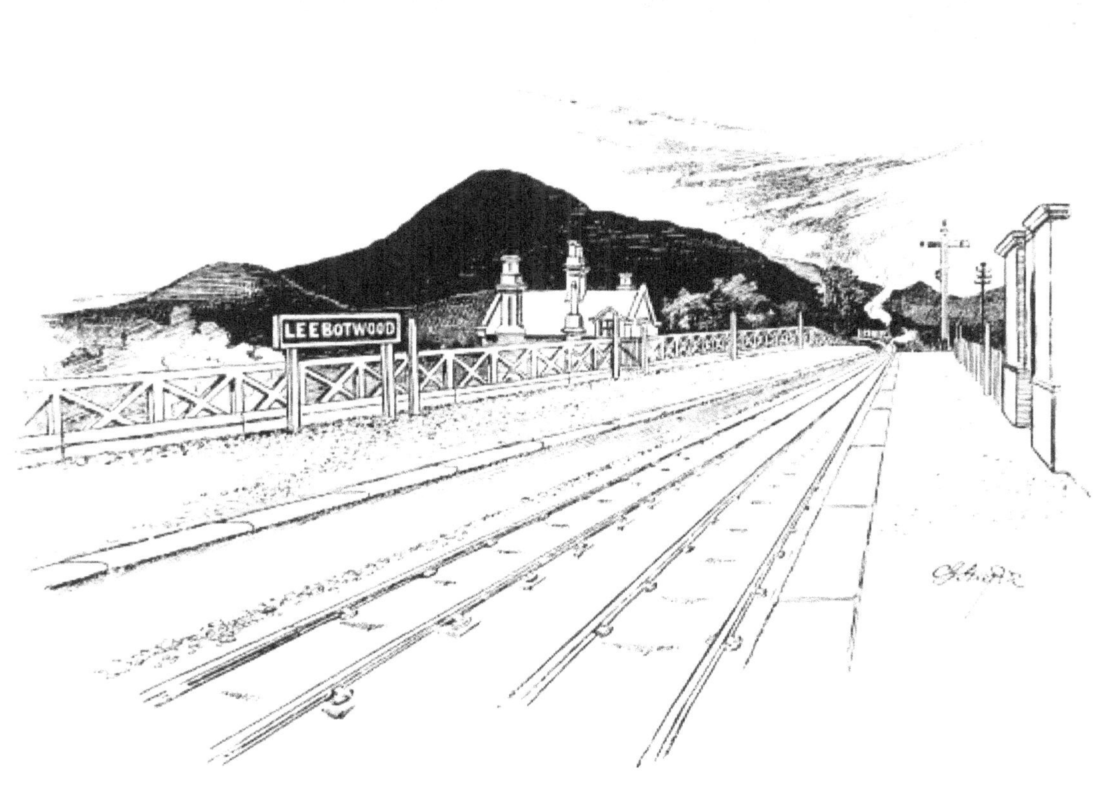

11½ × 8¾.   LEEBOTWOOD.

Showing application of shading medium to treatment of sky.

These tints are produced by Day's shading mediums; thin sheets of gelatine engraved upon one side with lines or with a pattern of stipple. There are very many of these patterns. They can readily be applied, and with the greatest accuracy, because the gelatine is semi-transparent, and admits of the operator seeing what he is about. These mechanical tints are capable of exquisite application, but they have been more frequently regarded as labour-saving appliances, and have rarely been used with skill, and so have come to bear an altogether unmerited stigma. They can be used by a clever process-man, under the directions of the draughtsman, with great effect, and in remarkably diverse ways. For it is not at all necessary that the tint should come all over the block. It can be worked in most intricately. The illustration, *Leebotwood*, shows an application of shading medium to the sky. The proprietors (for it is a patent) of these devices have endeavoured to introduce their use amongst artists, with a view to their working the mediums upon the drawings themselves. It has been shown that the varieties of shading to be obtained by shifting and transposing the gelatine plates is illimitable, but as their use involves establishing a printing roller and printer's ink in one's studio, and as all artists are not printers born, it does not seem at all likely that Day's shading mediums will be used outside lithographic offices or the offices of reproductive firms.

The cost of reproduction by process varies very greatly. It is always calculated at so much the square inch, with a minimum charge ranging, for line-work, from two-and-sixpence to five shillings. For half-tone the minimum may be put at from ten shillings to sixteen shillings. Plain line blocks, by the bitumen or albumen processes, cost from twopence-halfpenny to sixpence per square inch, and handwork upon the block is charged extra. Some firms make a charge of one penny per square inch for the application of Day's shading mediums. Line blocks by the swelled gelatine process are charged at one shilling per square inch, and reproductions of pencil or crayon work at one-and-threepence. Half-tone blocks from objects, photographs, or drawings range from eightpence to one-and-sixpence per square inch, and the cost of a photogravure plate may be put at two-and-sixpence for the same unit. The best work in any photographic process is infinitely less costly than wood engraving, which, although its cost is not generally calculated on the basis of the inch, as in all process work, may range approximately from three shillings to five shillings for engraving of average merit.

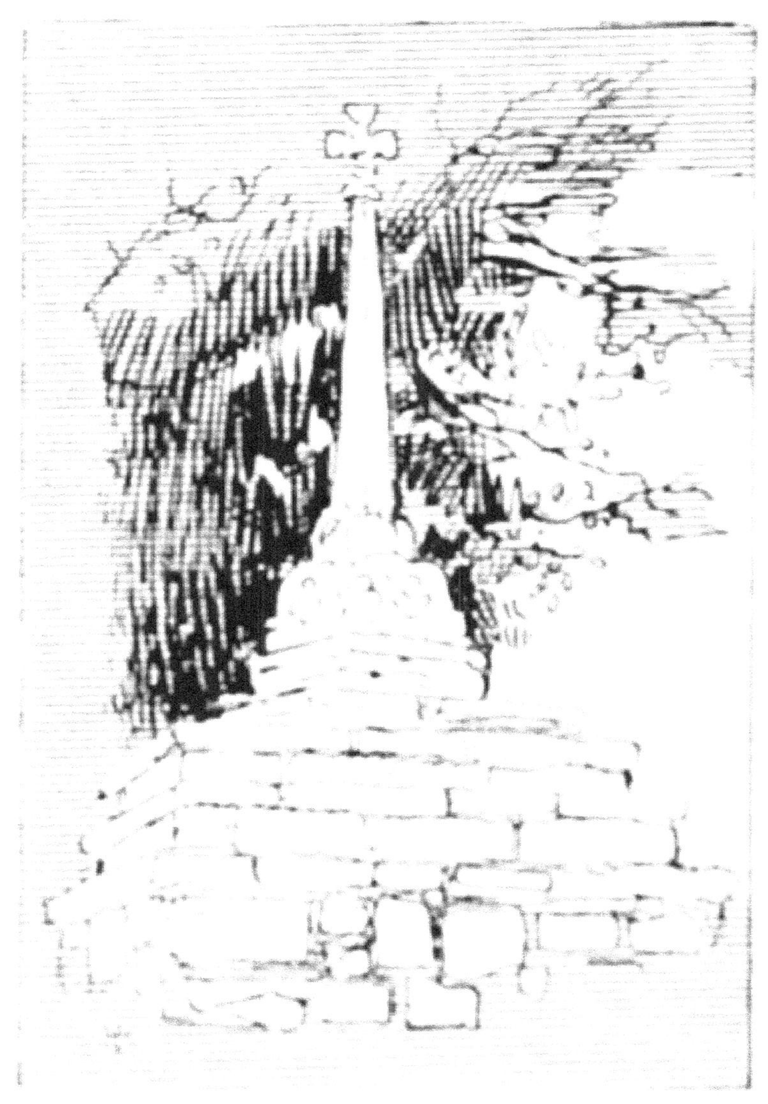

CHURCHYARD CROSS, RAGLAN.
Application of shading medium.

Electrotype copies of line blocks cost from three-farthings to three-halfpence per square inch, and from half-tone blocks, twopence, although it is not advisable to have electrotypes taken of these fine and delicate blocks. If duplicates are wanted of half-tones, the usual practice is to have two original blocks made, the process-engraver charging for the second block half the price of the first.

PAPER.

The process engraver will tell you, if you seek counsel of him, that you should use Bristol-board, and of that only the smoothest and most highly finished varieties. But, however easy it may render his work of reproduction, there is no necessity for you to draw upon cardboard or smooth-surfaced paper at all. Paper of a reasonable whiteness is, of course, necessary to any process of line engraving which has photography as a basis, but to say that stiff cardboards or papers of a blue-white, as opposed to the cream-laid variety, are necessary is merely to obscure what is, after all, a simple matter.

Bristol-board is certainly a very favourite material, and the varieties of cardboards sold under that name are numerous enough to please anybody. Goodall's sell as reliable a make as can be readily found. It is white enough to please the photo-engraver, and of a smooth, hard surface; and a hard surface you must have for pen-work. But it is an unsympathetic material, and it is an appreciably more difficult matter to make a pencil sketch upon it than upon such papers as Whatman's HP.

Mounting-boards are frequently used, chiefly for journalistic pen-work, when it may be supposed nobody cares anything about the *finesse* of the art, but only that the drawing shall be up to a certain standard of excellence, and, more particularly, up to time. Mounting-boards are appreciably cheaper than good Bristol-board, but if erasures are to be made they are troublesome, because under the surface they are composed of the shoddiest of matter. They are convenient, indeed admirable, for studies carried out in a masculine manner with a quill pen, or for simple drawings made with an ordinary writing nib, with not too sharp a point. For delicate technique they are not to be recommended.

Indeed, for anything but work done at home, cardboards of any sort are inexpedient; they are heavy, and take up too much space. If they were necessary, of course you would have to put up with the inconvenience of carrying two or more pounds' weight of them about with you, but they are not necessary.

Every one who makes drawings in pen and ink is continually looking out for an ideal paper; many have found their ideals in this respect; but that paper which one man swears by, another will, not inconceivably, swear at, so no recommendation can be trusted. Again, personal predilections change amazingly. One day you will be able to use Bristol-board with every satisfaction; another, you will find its smooth, dead white, immaculate surface perfectly dispiriting. No one's advice can be implicitly followed in respect of papers, inks, or pens. Every one must find his own especial fancy, and when he has found it he will produce the better work.

The pen-draughtsman who is a paper-fancier does not leave untried even the fly-leaves of his correspondence. Papers have been found in this way which have proved satisfactory. All you have to do is to go to some large stationer or wholesale papermaker's and get your fancy matched. It would be an easy matter to obtain sheets larger than note-paper.

Whatman's HP, or hot-pressed drawing-paper, is good for pen-drawing, but its proper use is not very readily learnt. To begin with, the surface is full of little granulations and occasional fibres which catch the pen and cause splutterings and blots. Sometimes, too, you happen upon insufficiently sized Whatman, and then lines thicken almost as if the drawing were being made upon blotting-paper.

A good plan is to select some good HP Whatman and have it calendered. Any good stationer could put you in the way of getting the calendering done, or possibly such a firm as Dickinsons', manufacturers of paper, in Old Bailey, could be prevailed upon to do it. If you want a firm, hard, clear-cut line, you will of course use only Bristol-board or mounting-board, or papers with a highly finished surface. Drawings upon Whatman's papers give in the reproductions broken and granulated lines which the process-man (but no one else) regards as defects. Should the block itself be defective, he will doubtless point to the paper as the cause, but there is no reason why the best results should not proceed from HP paper. Messrs. Reeves and Sons, of Cheapside, sell what they call London boards. These are sheets of Whatman mounted upon cardboard. They offer the advantages of the HP surface with the rigidity of the Bristol-board. The Art Tablets sold by the same firm are cardboards with Whatman paper mounted on either side. A drawing can be made upon both sides and the tablet split up afterwards.

In connection with illustration, amongst the most remarkable inventions of late years are the prepared cardboards generally known amongst illustrators as "scratch-out cardboards," introduced by Messrs. Angerer and Göschl of Vienna, and by M. Gillot of Paris. These cardboards are of several kinds, but are all prepared with a surface of kaolin, or china-clay. Reeves sell eight varieties of these clay-boards. They are somewhat expensive, costing two shillings a sheet of nineteen by thirteen inches, but when their use is well understood they justify their existence by the rich effects obtained, and by the saving of time effected in drawing upon them. Drawings made upon these preparations have all the fulness and richness of wash, pencil, or crayon, and may be reproduced by line processes at the same cost as a pen-drawing made upon plain paper. The simplest variety of clay-board is the one prepared with a plain white surface, upon which a drawing may be made with pen and ink, or with a brush, the lights taken out with a scraper or a sharp-pointed knife. It is advisable to work upon all clay-surfaced papers or cardboards with pigmental inks, as, for instance, lampblack, ivory-black, or Indian ink. Ebony stain is not suitable. The more liquid inks and stains have a tendency to soak *through* the prepared surface of china-clay, rather than to rest only *upon* it, thereby rendering the cardboard useless for "scratch-out" purposes, and of no more value than ordinary drawing-paper. A drawing made upon plain clay-board with pen and brush, using lampblack as a medium, can be worked upon very effectively with a sharp point. White lines of a character not to be obtained in any other way can be thus produced with happy effect. Mr. Heywood Sumner has made some of his most striking decorative drawings in this manner. It is a manner of working remarkably akin to the wood-engraver's art—that is to say, drawing or engraving in white lines upon a black field— only of course the cardboard is more readily worked upon than the wood block. Indeed, wood-engravers have frequently used this plain clay-board. They have had the surface sensitized, the drawing photographed and printed upon it, and have then proceeded to take out lights, to cut out white lines, and to hatch and cross-hatch, until the result looks in every way similar to a wood engraving. This has then been photographed again, and a zinc block made that in the printing would defy even an expert to detect.

Other kinds of clay-boards are impressed with a grain or with plain indented lines, or printed upon with black lines or reticulations, which may be scratched through with a point, or worked upon with brush or pen. Examples are given here:

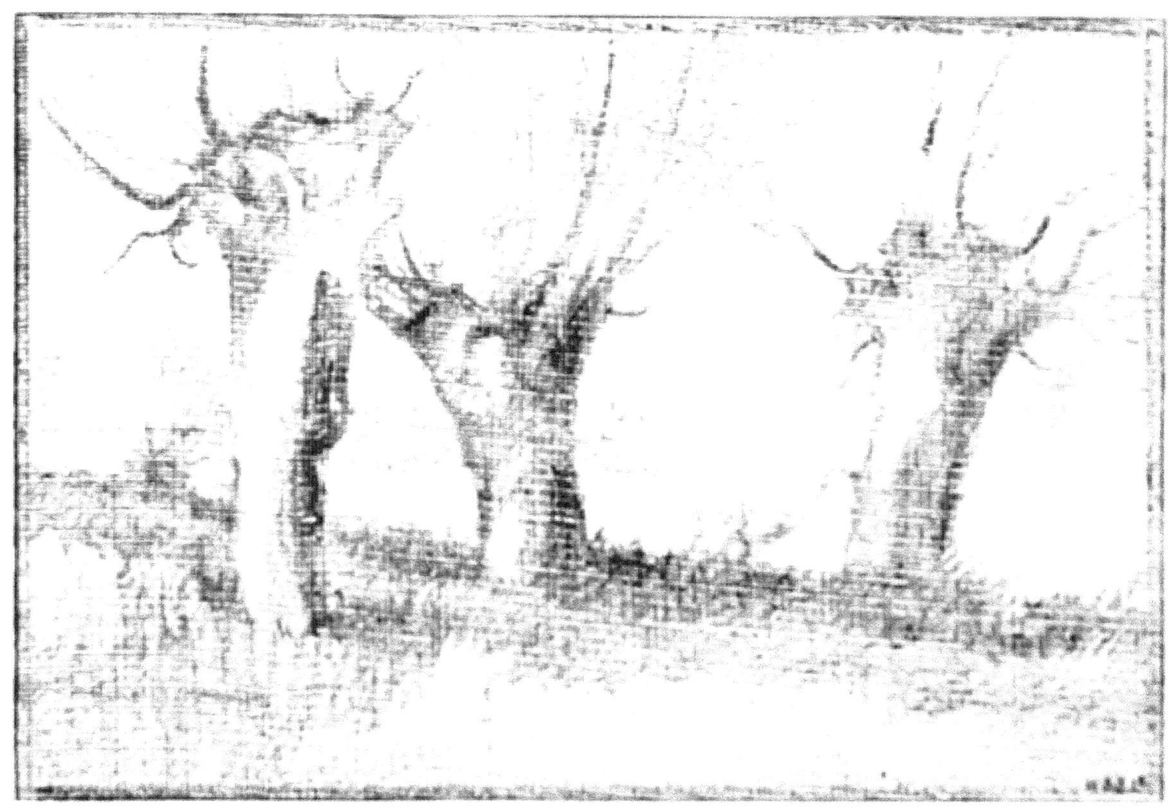

CANVAS-GRAIN CLAY-BOARD.

No. 1. White cardboard, impressed with a plain canvas grain.

This gives a fine painty effect, as shown in the drawing of polled willows: a drawing made in pencil, with lights in foreground grass and on tree-trunks scratched out with a knife or with the curved-bladed eraser sold for use with these preparations.

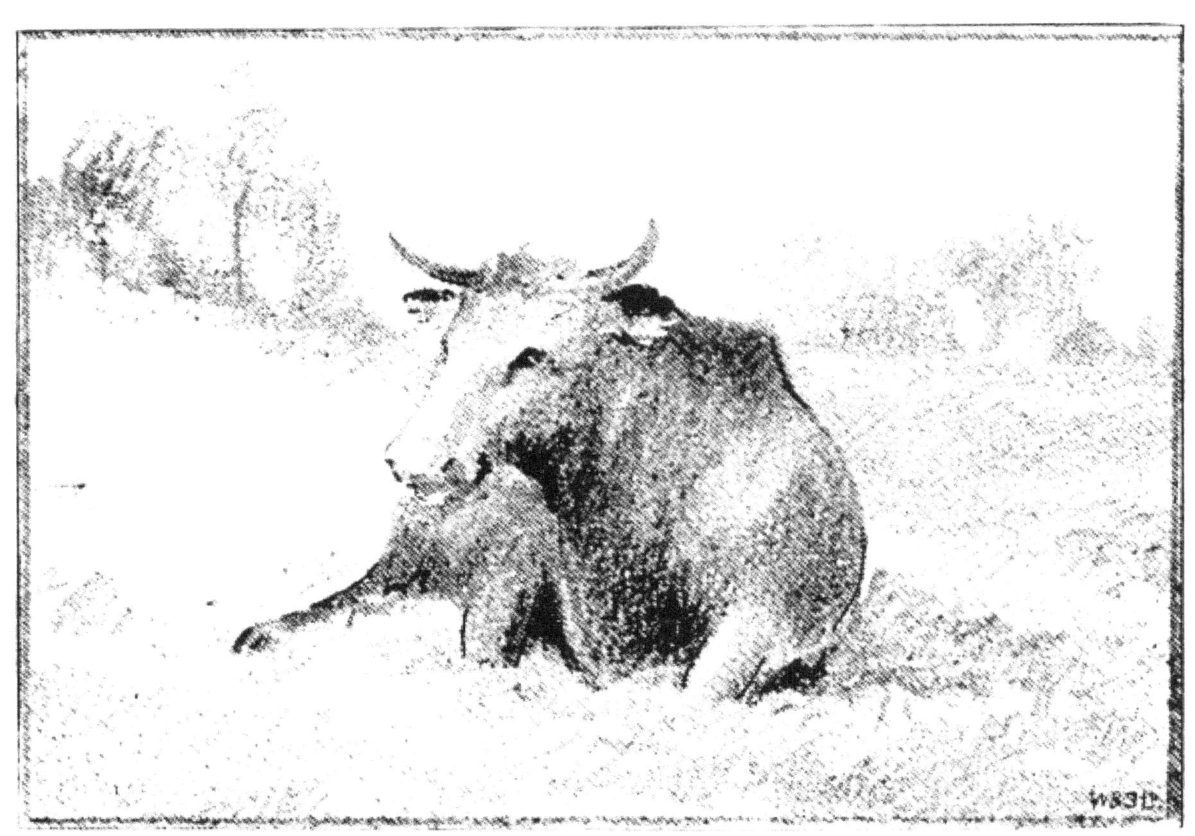

PLAIN DIAGONAL GRAIN.

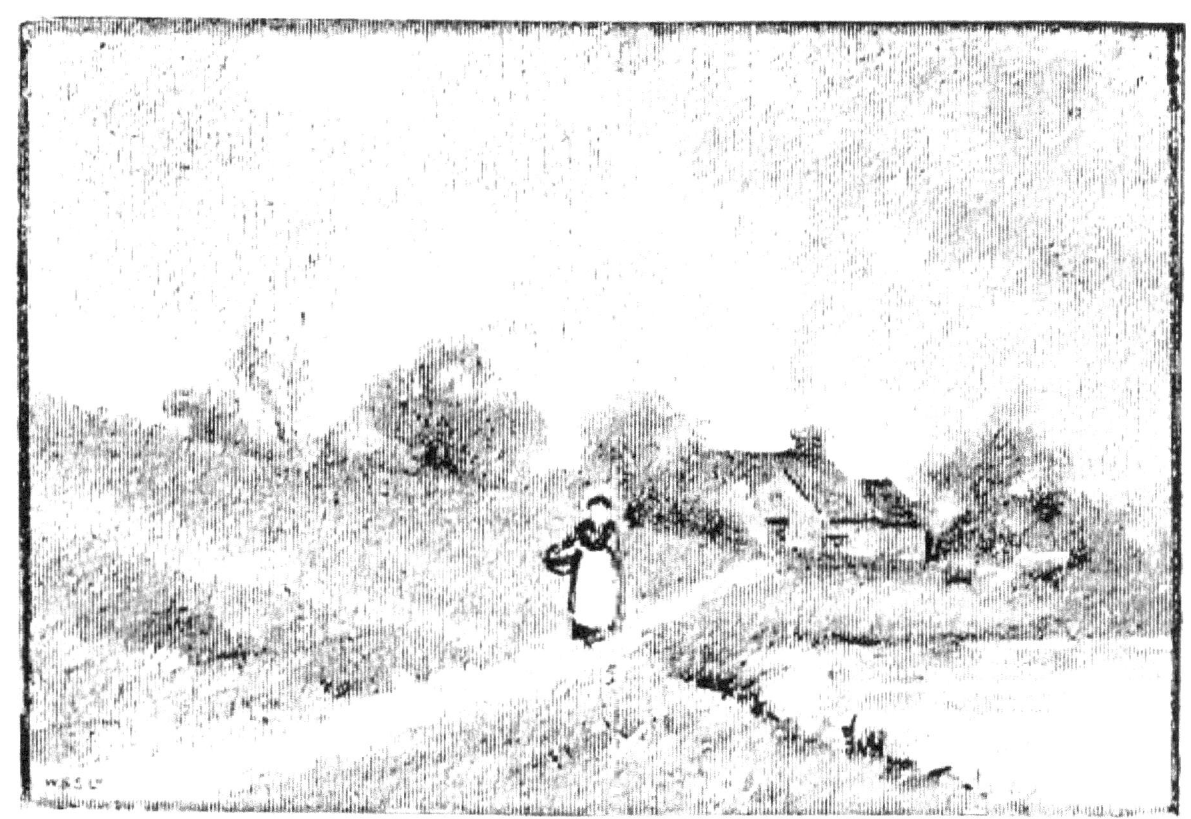

PLAIN PERPENDICULAR GRAIN.

2. <u>Plain white diagonal lines</u>. Pencil drawing.

3. <u>Plain white perpendicular lines</u>. Pencil drawing.

4. <u>Plain white aquatint grain</u>. Pencil drawing.

These four varieties require greater care and a lighter hand in working than the others, because their patterns are not very deeply stamped, and consequently the furrows between the upstanding lines are apt to become filled with pencil, and to give a broken and spotty effect in the reproduction.

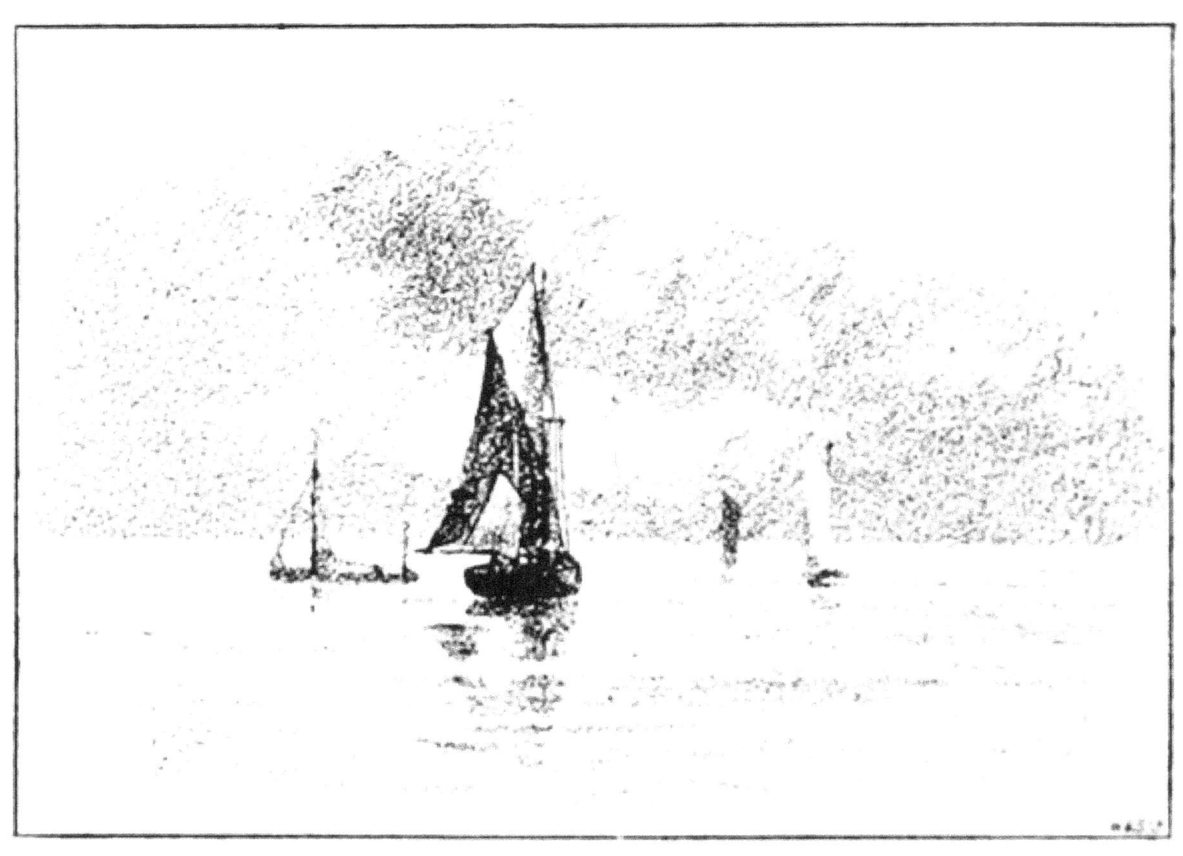

DRAWING IN PENCIL ON WHITE AQUATINT GRAIN CLAY-
BOARD.

5. Black aquatint. This is not a variety in constant use. Three states are shown.

6. Black diagonal lines. This is the pattern in greater requisition. The method of working is shown, but the possibilities of this pattern are seen admirably and to the best advantage in the illustration of *Venetian Fête on the Seine*.

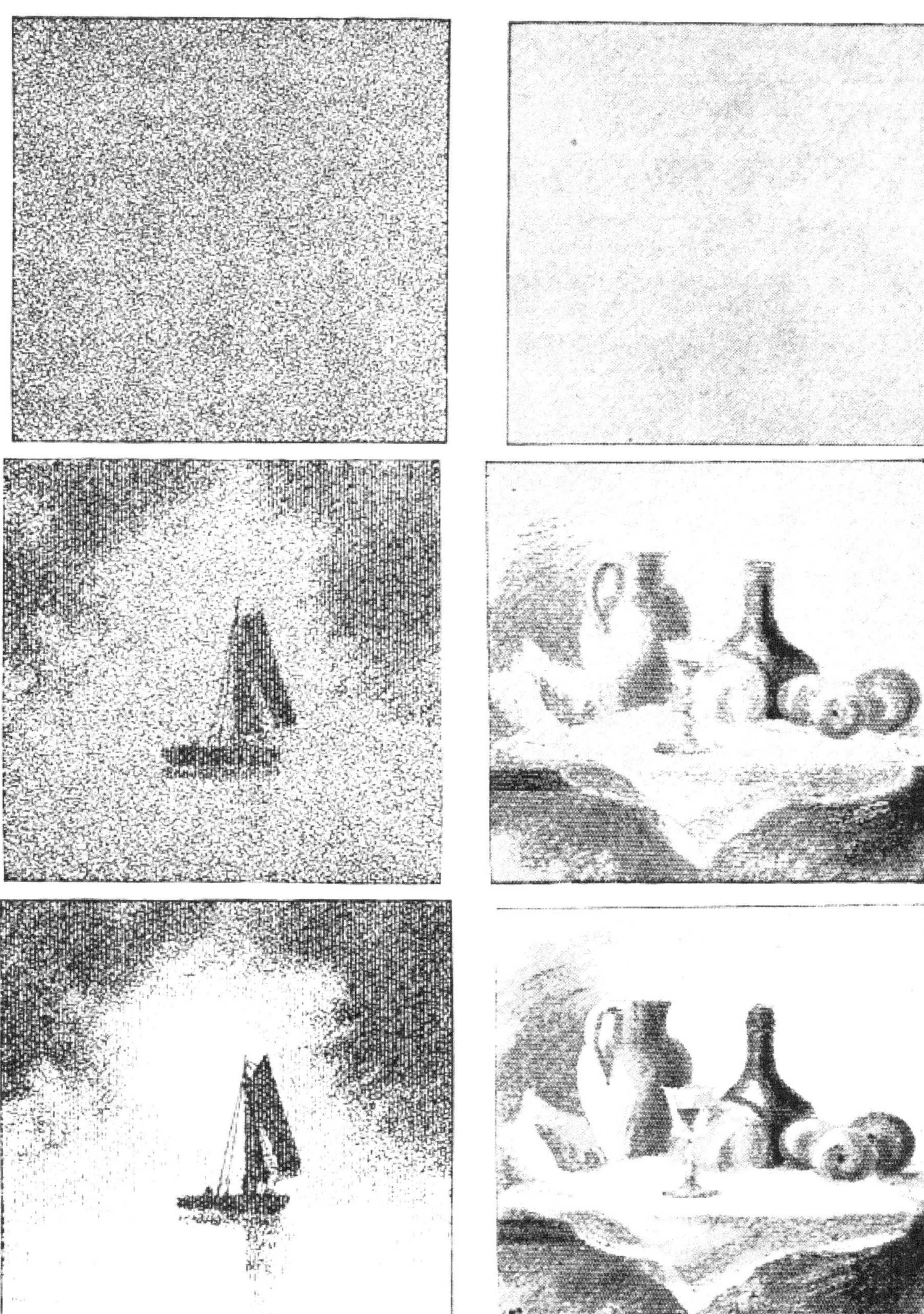

7. <u>Black perpendicular lines</u>. Same as <u>No. 6</u>, except in direction of line.

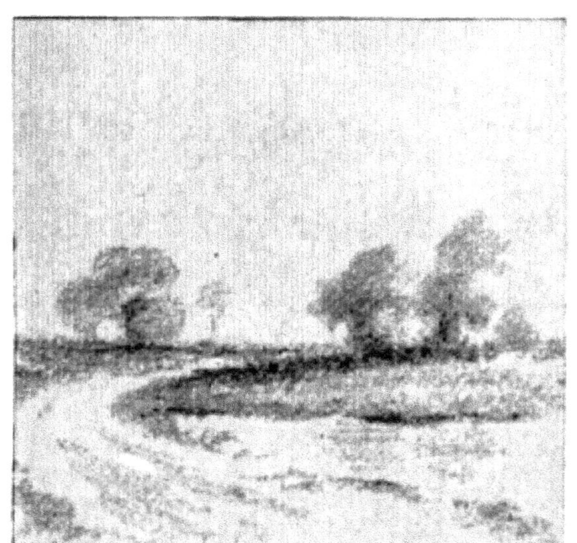

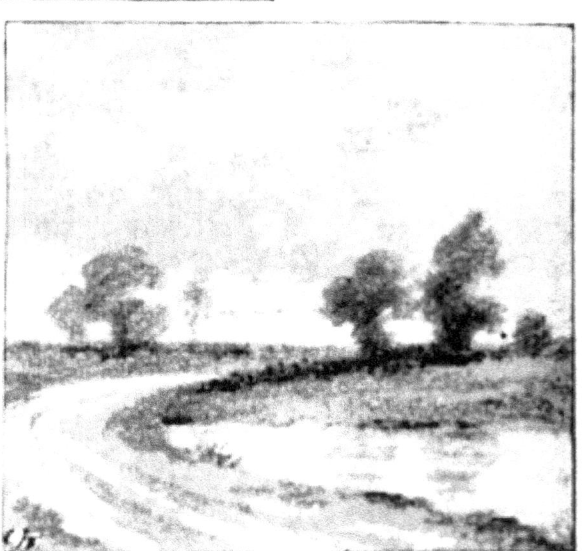

BLACK PERPENDICULAR-LINED CLAY-BOARD AND TWO
STAGES OF DRAWING.

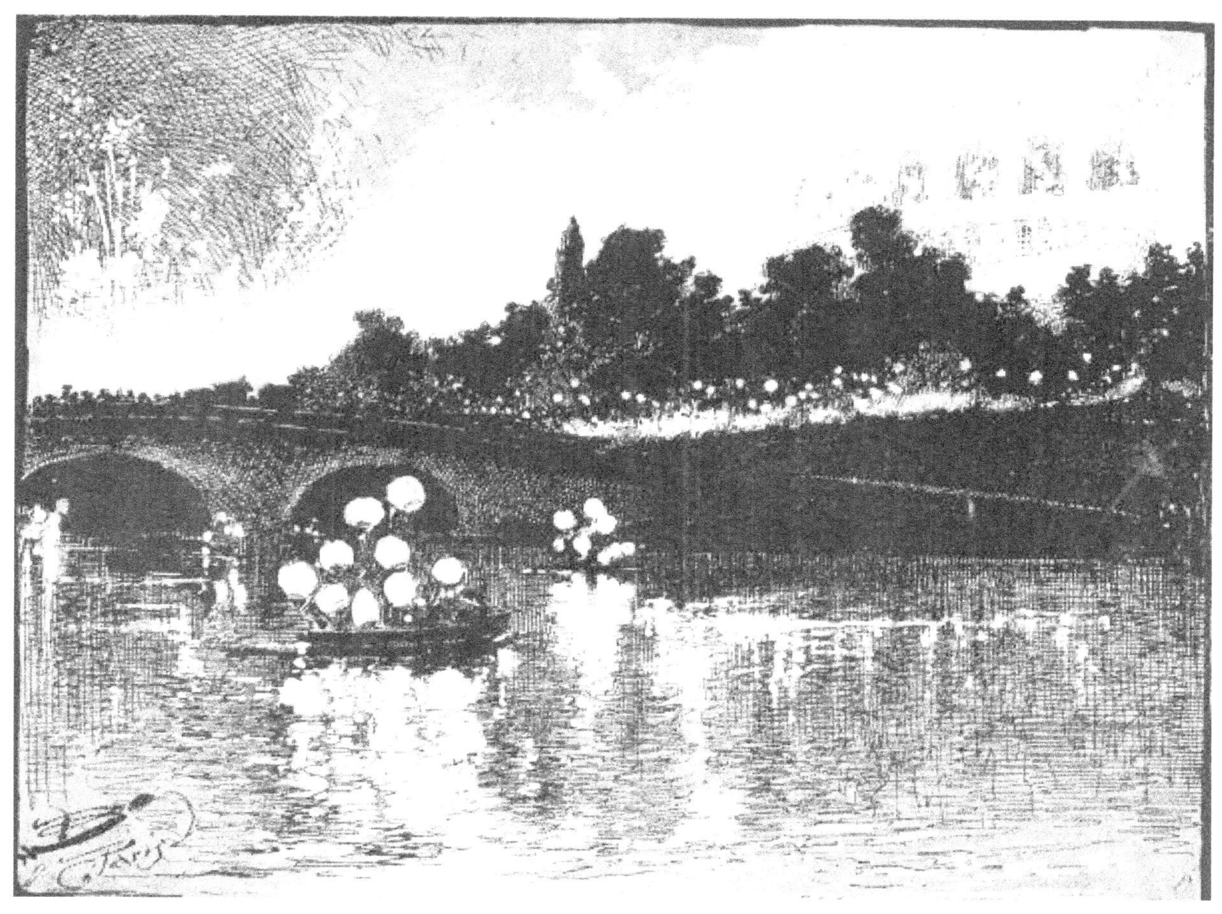

VENETIAN FÊTE ON THE SEINE, WITH THE TROCADERO
ILLUMINATED.

Pen and ink on black diagonal-lined clay-board. Lights scratched out.

Drawings made upon these grained and ridged papers must not be stumped down or treated in any way that would fill up the interstices, which give the lined and granular effect capable of reproduction by line-process. Also, it is very important to note that drawings on these papers can only be subjected to a slight reduction of scale—say, a reduction at most by one quarter. The closeness of the printed grains and lines forbids a smaller scale that shall be perfect. Mr. C. H. Shannon has drawn upon lined "scratch-out" cardboard with the happiest effect.

PENS.

A common delusion as to pens for drawing is that only the finer-pointed kinds are suitable. To the contrary, most of the so-called "etching pens" and crow-quills and lilliputian affairs sold are not only unnecessary, but positively harmful. They encourage the niggling methods of the amateur, and are, besides, untrustworthy and dreadfully scratchy. You can but rarely depend upon them for the drawing of a continuous line; frequently they refuse to mark at all. I know very well that I shall be exclaimed against when I say that a good medium-pointed pen or fine-pointed school nib are far better than three-fourths of the pens especially made for draughtsmen, but that is the case.

With practice, one can use almost any writing nib for the production of a pen-drawing. Even the broad-pointed J pen is useful. Quill pens are delightful to work with for the making of pen-studies in a bold, free manner. A well-cut quill flies over all descriptions of paper, rough or smooth, without the least catching of fibres or spluttering. It is the freest and least trammelling of pens, and seems almost to draw of its own volition.

Brandauer's pens are, generally, very good, chiefly for the reason that they have circular points that rarely become scratchy. They make a small nib, No. 515, which works and wears well; this last an unusual quality in the small makes. Perry & Co. sell two very similar nibs, No. 601 (a so-called "etching pen") and No. 25; they are both scratchy. Gillott's crowquill, No. 659, is a barrel pen, very small and very good, flexible, and capable of producing at once the finest and the boldest lines; but Brandauer's Oriental pen, No. 342 EF, an ordinary fine-pointed writing pen, is just as excellent, and its use is more readily learnt. It takes some time and practice to discover the capabilities of the Gillott crowquill; the other pen's possibilities are easier found. Besides, the tendency with a microscopic nib is to niggled work, which is not to be desired at the cost of vigour. Mitchell's F pen is a fine-pointed school writing nib. It is not particularly flexible, but very reliable and lasts long. Gillott has recently introduced a very remarkable nib, No. 1000, frankly a drawing pen, flexible in the extreme, capable of producing at will the finest of hair-lines or the broadest of strokes.

Some illustrators make line drawings with a brush. Mr. J. F. Sullivan works in this way, using a red sable brush with all superfluous hairs cut away, and fashioned to a point. Lampblack is the best medium for the brush.

To draw in line with a brush requires long practice and great dexterity, but men who habitually work in this way say that its use once learnt, no one would exchange it for the pen. Of this I can express no opinion. Certainly there are some obvious advantages in using a brush. It does not ever penetrate the surface of the paper, and it is capable of producing the most solid and smooth lines.

Stylographic and fountain pens, of whatever make, are of no use whatever. Glass pens are recommended by some draughtsmen for their quality of drawing an equable line; but they would seem to be chiefly useful in mathematical and engineering work, which demands the same thickness of line throughout. These pens would also prove very useful in architects' offices, in drawing profiles of mouldings, tracery, and crockets, because, not being divided into two nibs, they make any variety of curve without the slightest alteration in the character of the line produced. Any one accustomed to use the ordinary divided nibs will know the difficulty of drawing such curves with them.

INKS.

It is, perhaps, more difficult to come by a thoroughly reliable ink than to be exactly suited with papers and pens; and yet greater attention has been given by manufacturers to inks than to those other necessaries.

You can, often with advantage, use a writing pen; but no one, however clever he may be, can make a satisfactory drawing for reproduction with the aid of writing-inks. They are either not black enough, or else are too fluid, so that it is impossible to run lines close together, or to cross-hatch without the ink running the lines into one another. It may, perhaps, be remarked that this is an obvious error, since many of Keene's most delightful drawings and studies were made in writing-inks—black, blue-black, or diluted, or even in red, and violet, and blue inks. Certainly Keene was a great man in whatever medium he used, but he was not accustomed to be reproduced in any other way than by so-called *fac-simile* wood engraving. In this way all his greynesses and faint lines could have their relative values translated, but even in the cleverest surface-printing processes his work could not be adequately reproduced.

Stephens's ebony stain is perhaps the most widely used ink at this time. It is not made for the purpose of drawing, being a stain for wood; but its merits for pen-drawing have been known for some considerable time. It is certainly the best, cheapest, and least troublesome medium in the market. It is, when not diluted, an intensely black liquid with an appreciable body, but not too thick to flow freely. It dries with a certain but not very obtrusive glaze, which process-engravers at one time objected to most strongly, *because* they wanted something to object to on principle; but they have at length become tired of remonstrating, and really there was never any objection to the stain upon that score. It flows readily from the pen, and when drying upon the nib is not gummy nor in any way adhesive, but powders easily—avoiding the abomination of a pen clogged with a sticky mess of half-dry mud, characteristic of the use of Indian ink. Ebony stain is sold in substantial stone bottles, and so does not readily become thick; but when, owing to any cause, it does not run freely enough, a sparing dilution with water restores its fluid properties. Diluted too often or too freely, it becomes of a decided purple-brown tint; but as a good-sized bottle costs only sixpence, and holds enough to last a year, it need not be repeatedly diluted on the score of its cost. It is not a fixed ink, and readily smudges when washed over or spotted with water—so cannot be used in combination with water-colour or flat-washes. Neither can Chinese white be used upon a drawing made in Ebony stain. These are disadvantages that would tell against its use by illustrators who make many alterations upon their work, or who paint in lights on a pen-drawing with body-colour; but for pure pen-drawing, and for straight-away journalistic work, it is invaluable.

Indian ink is the traditional medium. It has the advantage of fixity; lines drawn with it, when once dry, will not smudge when washed over, and, at most, they give but a very slight grey or brown tint to the paper. Indian ink can be bought in sticks and ground with water in a saucer; but there seems to be no reason for any one to go to this trouble, as liquid Indian inks are to be bought in bottles from Messrs. Reeves. The best Indian ink, when freshly ground, gives a fine black line that dries with that bogey of the process-man, a glaze; but lampblack is of a more intense blackness, and dries with a dull surface. Lampblack is easily soluble, and therefore has not the stability of good Indian ink to recommend it. For ordinary use with the pen, it has too much of the pigmental nature, and is very apt to clog the nib and to cause annoyance and loss of time. Lampblack and Ivory-black are better suited to the brush. Hentschel, of 182, Fleet Street, sells an American preparation called "Whiting's Process-Drawing Ink," which professes to have all the virtues that should accompany a drawing-ink. It is very abominable, and has an immediate corrosive effect upon pens. The drawing-materials' shop in King William Street, Strand, sells "Higgins' American Drawing Ink," done up in ingeniously contrived bottles. It is well spoken of.

Encre de Chine Liquide is the best liquid Indian ink sold, and is very largely used by draughtsmen. It can be obtained readily at any good colour-shop. It is far preferable to most of the liquid Indian inks prepared by English houses, which when left standing for a few minutes deposit a sediment, and at best are inadequate concoctions of a greenish-grey colour. Messrs. Reeves and Sons have recently introduced a special ink for pen-drawing, which they call "Artists' Black." It is as good as any. It is a liquid ink, sold in shilling bottles.

Mr. Du Maurier uses blue-black writing-ink from an inkstand that is always allowed to stand open and receive dust and become half muddy. He prefers it in this condition. Also he generally works upon HP drawing-paper. It is interesting to know this, but to work in blue-black ink is an amiable eccentricity that might prove disastrous to any one following his example. His work is not reproduced by zincography, but by *fac-simile* wood engraving. It may be laid down as an inflexible rule, if you are beginning the study of pen-drawing, if your work is for hurried newspaper production, or if you have not the control of the reproduction in your own hands, to draw for line-process in the blackest ink and on the whitest paper.

Many architects and architectural draughtsmen, who are accustomed to exhibit pen-drawings of architecture at the Royal Academy, are accustomed to draw in brown inks. Prout's Brown is generally used, and gives a very pleasing effect to a drawing. It photographs and reproduces readily, but it must always be borne in mind that, if printed in black ink, the reproduction will inevitably be much heavier. Scarlet inks, and even yellow inks, have been used by draughtsmen for special purposes, and are allowable from the photographic point of view; but blue must not be used, being an actinic colour and impossible to photograph.

THE MAKING OF A PEN-DRAWING.

It is not to be supposed that because the pen is so handy an instrument, and inks and paper, of sorts, are everywhere, that the making of a pen-drawing is a simple affair of a few uneducated strokes. The less you know of the art, the easier it seems, and they do but show their ignorance who speak of its simplicity. You will want as much power of draughtsmanship, and more, for drawing in this medium than in many others; because the difference between good drawing and bad is more readily seen in line-work than in other methods, and since in these days the standard of the art has been raised so high. You will want not less study in the open air, or with the life-class for figure-work, than the painter gives or should give to his preliminary studies for his art. This drudgery you will have to go through, whether in the schools of the Science and Art Department (which does not recognize this, the livest art of our time), or in the studio and under the care of some artist who receives pupils in the fashion of the *atélier* system in France. But such studios are rare in England. It seems likely that the student of pen-drawing, who starts with learning draughtsmanship of any sort, must first go through much of the ordinary grind of the schools, and, when he has got some sort of proficiency, turn to and worry out the application of the pen to his already received teaching. No one will teach him pen-drawing as an individual art; of that there is no doubt. Perhaps the best course he could pursue would be to become acquainted with the books illustrated by the foremost men, and study them awhile to see in what manner they work with the pen, and with this knowledge set to work with models, in the same way as a painter would do. Or, if your work is of another branch beside the figure, go to the fields, the hedgerows, and all the glory of the country-side, and work first-hand. The sketch-book is a necessity, and should always be in the student's pocket for the jotting down of notes and memoranda.

I do not think many pen-draughtsmen are careful enough to make a thorough pencil study as the basis of their pen-drawing, although that is the best way to proceed, and their drawings would be all the better for the practice. It is to this absence of the preliminary pencil-work, this shirking of an undoubted drudgery, that is due the quantity of uninspired, fumbling drawing with the pen that we see nowadays. The omission of a carefully made original pencil-sketch, over which to work in pen and ink, renders commonplace the work of many artists which, if only they were less impatient of toil, would become transfigured. What is so injurious to the man who has learnt his art is fatal to one who is by way of beginning its study. Make, then, a pencil-drawing in outline, using an HB pencil, as carefully as if that only were the end and object of your work. Work lightly with this hard pencil upon the paper or cardboard you have selected, indicating shadows rather than filling them in. It is necessary to make only faint pencil lines, for they will have to be rubbed out eventually, after the pen-drawing has been made over them. If the marks were deep and strong, a great deal of rubbing would have to be done to get them out, and that injures the surface of the paper and greys the black lines of the ink used. On the other hand, if the pencil-marks were not rubbed out, they would very likely photograph and reproduce in the process-block. To a pen-draughtsman of experience the reproduction of his pencil-marks can be made an additional beauty; but the student had much better be, at first, a purist, and make for clean pen-strokes alone on his finished drawing.

It must always be remembered, if you are working for reproduction (and consequent reduction of scale from the drawing to the process-block), that the pen-work you have seen printed in the books and papers and magazines was made on a much larger scale than you see it reproduced in their pages. Very frequently, as in the American magazines, the reduction is to about one quarter scale of the original drawing; but, working for process in England, the drawing should, generally speaking, be from two-thirds to one-half larger than the reproduction. These proportions will, as a rule, give excellent results.

Seeing that your drawing is to be so much larger than the process-block, it follows that the pen-work can, with advantage, be correspondingly vigorous. It would help you better than any description to a notion of what an original drawing should be like, if you could obtain a glance at the originals of any good pen-draughtsmen. But unfortunately, there are few exhibitions in which pen-work has any place.

When your pencil study is completed in an outline giving all details down to the minutest, you can set about the pen-drawing. Often, indeed, if carefully made, the pencil-sketch looks too good to be covered up with ink.

If you wish to retain it, it can, if made upon thin paper, be traced upon cardboard with the aid of black carbon paper, or better still (since blue will not photograph) with blue transfer paper, which you can either purchase or make for yourself by taking thin smooth paper and rubbing powdered blue chalk upon one side of it, or scribbling closely upon it with blue pencil. There is another way of tracing the pencil-drawing: by pinning over it a sheet of thin correspondence paper (of the kind called Bank Post) and working upon that straight away.

But, after all, it would, for the sake of retaining something of the freshness of first impressions, be best to sacrifice your pencil study and work away on that.

Now the pen-drawing is begun, care should be taken to draw only clear and perfectly black lines, and not to run these together, but to keep the drawing what the process men call "open."

If details are put in without regard for the fining down which reduction gives, it is only too likely that the result will show only dirty, meaningless patches where was a great deal of delicate pen-work. Of course, the exact knowledge of how to draw with the pen to get the best results by process cannot properly be taught, but must be learned by experience, after many miscalculations.

It will be found, too, that many things which it would be inadvisable for the beginner to do (especially if he cannot command his own choice of process-engraver) are perfectly legitimate to the practised artist who has studied process work. The student should not be at first encouraged to make experiments in diluted inks or retained pencil-marks, or any of those delightful practices by which one who is thoroughly conversant with photographic processes and pen-drawing varies the monotony of his medium. He should begin by making his drawings as simply as he can, so that they express his subject. And this simplicity, this quality of suggestion, is the true field of pen-work. The best work is reticent and sober, giving the greatest number of essential facts in the fewest strokes. If you can express a fact with sufficient intelligibility in half a dozen pen strokes, it is inartistic and inexpedient to worry it into any number of scratches. This is often done because the public likes to see that there has been plenty of manual labour put into the work it buys. It is greatly impressed with the knowledge that any particular drawing took days to complete, and it respects that drawing accordingly, and has nothing but contempt for a sketch which may have taken only an hour or so, although the first may be artless and overloaded with unnecessary detail, and the second instinct with actuality and suggestion. But if you are drawing a landscape with a pen, that is no reason for putting in an elaborate foreground of grass, carefully working up each square inch. Such a subject can be rendered by a master in a few strokes, and though, possibly, you may never equal the artistry of the master, you can follow his ideals. Another and allied point in pen-and-ink art is its adaptability to what is termed "selection." You have, say, before you the view or object to be drawn. You do not need to make a drawing in which you shall niggle up every part of it, but you select (the trained eye readily does this) its salient feature and emphasize it and make it fall properly into the composition, leaving aught else either suggested or less thoroughly treated. Here is a pen-drawing made with a very special regard to a selection only of the essential. _The Gatehouse, Moynes Court_, is a singular structure near the shore of the Severn estuary, two miles below Chepstow. The singularity of its design, rarely paralleled in England, would give the artist the motive for sketching, and its tapering lines and curious roofs are best preserved in a drawing that deals chiefly in outline, and has but little shading wherewith to confuse the queer profile of these effective towers. This drawing was reproduced by the bitumen process. The lines in the foreground, suggestive of grass, were drawn in pencil. The pen-sketches and studies of the foremost artists which have been made, not for publication, but for practice, but which have sometimes been reproduced, as, for instance, some slight sketches of Charles Keene's, delight the artist's eye simply by reason of their suggestive and selective qualities. If you do not delight in these things, but have a desire to (as the untaught public might say) "see them finished," then it seems likely either that you have not the artistic sense, or else you have not sufficient training; but I should suspect you were in the first category, and should then advise you to leave matters artistic alone.

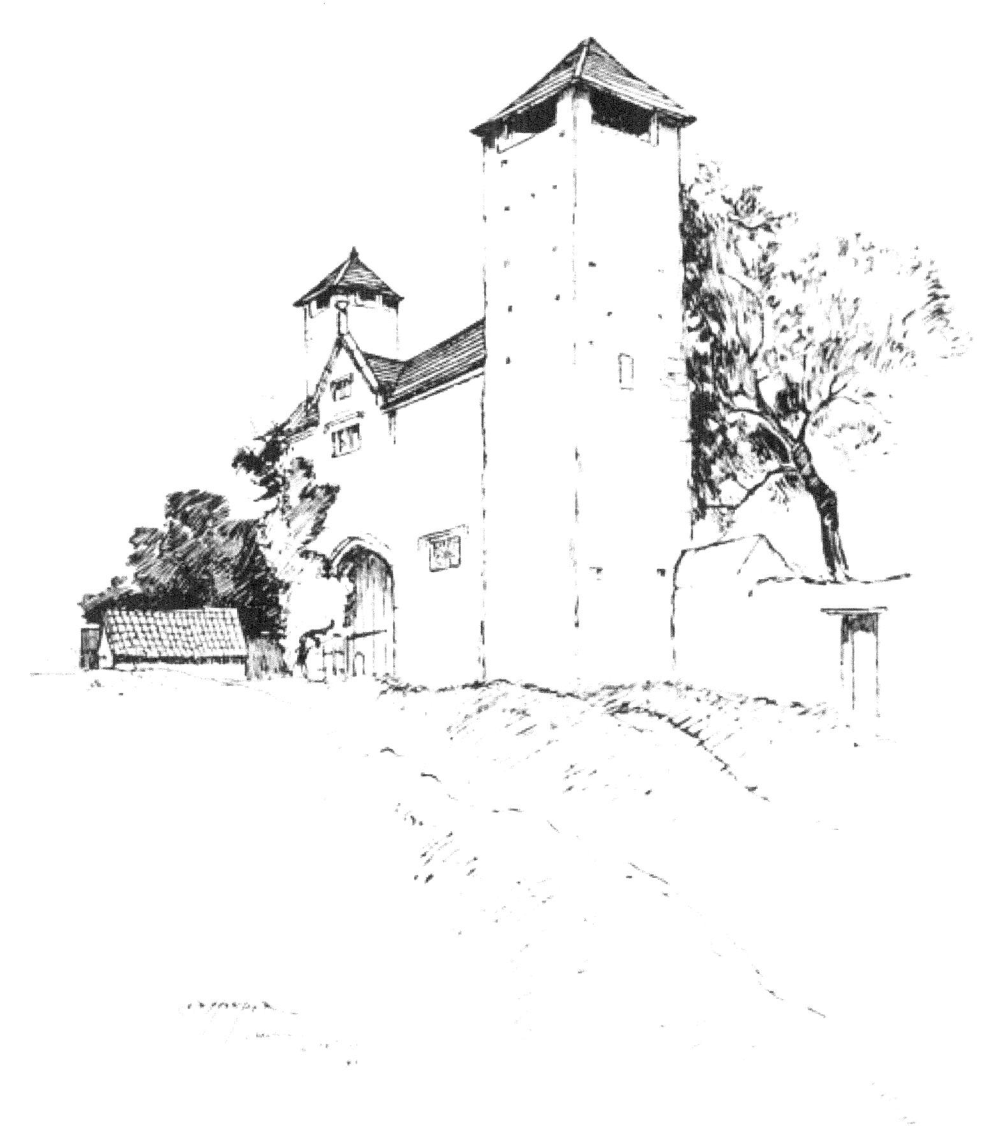

7¼ × 9.   THE GATEHOUSE, MOYNES COURT.

Bitumen process. Drawing showing value of selection.

You should not forget that in drawing for reproduction you are not working like the painter of a picture. The painter's picture exists for its own sake, not, like a pen or wash drawing, as only the means to an end. The end of these drawings is illustration, and when this is frankly acknowledged, no one has any right to criticize the neatness or untidiness of the means, so long as the end is kept properly in view.

We have not yet arrived at that stage of civilization when black-and-white art shall be appreciated as fully as colour. When we have won to that pinnacle of culture, then perhaps an original drawing in pen or monochrome will be cherished for its own sake; at present we are barbaric more than enough, and bright hues attract us only in lesser degree than our "friend and brother," Quashee from the Congo. How nearly related we are these preferences may show more readily than the ranter's impassioned oratory. As a drawing made for reproduction is only a stage on the way to the printed illustration, and is not the cynosure of collectors, it is successful or unsuccessful only in so far as it subserves this purpose. There is really no need for scrupulous neatness in the original; there is no necessity for it to have the appearance of a finished picture or of delicate execution, so only it will wear this appearance when reduced. That curious bugbear of neatness causes want of breadth and vigour, and is the cause of most of the tight and trammelled handling we see. Draughtsmen at the outset of their career are too much afraid of their mediums of white cardboard and ink, and too scrupulous in submitting their original drawings, beautifully cleaned up and trimmed round, to editors who, if they know their business, give no better consideration to them on that account. Mr. Ruskin has written, in his *Elements of Drawing*, some most misleading things with regard to drawing with the pen. True, his book was written in the '50's, before pen-drawing became an art, but it has been repeatedly reprinted even so lately as 1893, and consequently it is still actively dangerous. "Coarse art," *i.e.* bold work, says Mr. Ruskin—he is speaking of pen-drawing—"is always bad art." There you see Mr. Ruskin holding a brief for the British public which admires the ineffable artistry displayed in writing the Lord's Prayer on a threepenny piece, but deplores the immorality shown in drawings done with a quill pen. The art of a pen-drawing is *not* to be calculated on a sliding-scale graduated to microscopical fractions of an inch and applied to its individual strokes.

The appearance a drawing will present when reduced may be approximately judged by the use of a "diminishing glass," that is to say, a concave glass.

Drawings should not be cleaned up with india-rubber, which destroys the surface of paper or cardboard and renders lines rotten; bread should be used, preferably stale bread two days old, crumbled and rubbed over the drawing with the palm of the hand. Mr. Ruskin says that in this way "you waste the good bread, which is wrong;" but you had better use a handful of "the good bread" in this way than injure a good drawing.

The copying of wood engravings or steel prints, not for their subjects, but for their peculiar *techniques*, is a vicious and inartistic practice. Time used in this way is time wasted, and worse than wasted, because this practice is utterly at variance with the spirit of pen-work.

It is not a proof of artistry or consummate draughtsmanship to be able to draw a straight line or a perfect circle, the absurd legend of Giotto and his circle notwithstanding.

There are many labour-saving tricks in drawing for reproduction, but these have usually little connection with the purely artistic side of illustration. They have been devised chiefly to aid the new race of artist-journalists in drawing for the papers which cater for that well-known desire of the public to see its news illustrated hot and hot. Most of these methods and the larger proportion of the men who practice them are frankly journalistic, but some few draughtsmen have succeeded in resolving this sleight of hand into novel and interesting styles, and their hurried work has achieved a value all its own, scarcely legitimate, but aggressive and clamouring for attention.

One of these tricks in illustration is a method which is largely practised for journalistic illustration in America—drawing in pen and ink upon photographs, which are afterwards bleached out, the outline drawings remaining to be processed. Although not a desirable practice from an artistic point of view, it is advantageously used for news work or upon any occasion in which expedition is essential. The photograph to be treated in this way is printed by the usual silver-print method, with the exception that the paper used is somewhat differently prepared. What is known as "plain salted paper" is used; that is to say, paper prepared without the albumen which gives to ordinary silver-prints their smooth, shiny appearance. The paper is prepared by being soaked in a solution made by the following formula:—

Chlorate of ammonia	100 grains.
Gelatine	10 "
Water	10 ounces.

The print is made and fixed without toning. It may now be drawn upon with pen and Indian ink. The ink should be perfectly black and fixed. The drawing, if it is to be worth anything artistically, must not aim at anything like the fulness of detail which the photograph possesses. An outline drawing is readily made in this way, and a considerable amount of detail may be achieved. Indeed, the temptation is always to go over the photograph in pen and ink too fully, and only draughtsmen of accomplishment can resist this almost irresistible inducement to do too much. Still, admirable results have been obtained in this way by artists who know and practise the very great virtue of reticence.

When the drawing has been finished it is immersed in a solution of bichlorate of mercury dissolved in alcohol, which removes all traces of the photograph, leaving the drawing showing uninjured upon plain white paper. Omissions from the drawing may now be supplied and corrections made, and it is now ready for being processed. If very serious omissions are noticed, the photograph may be conjured back by immersing the paper in a solution of hyposulphite of soda.

Another and readier way is to draw upon photographs printed on ferro-prussiate paper. This paper may be purchased at any good photographic materials shop, or it can be prepared by brushing a sheet of paper over with a sensitizing solution composed of the two following solutions, A and B, prepared separately and then mixed in equal volumes:—

A	Citrate of iron and ammonia	1⅞ ounces.	
	Water	8	"
B	Ferricyanide of potassium	1¼	"
	Water	8	"

The paper must be prepared thus in a dark room and quickly dried. It will remain in good condition for three or four months, and is best preserved in a calcium tube. Prints made upon ferro-prussiate paper are formed in Prussian blue, and are fixed in the simplest way, on being taken from the printing frame, by washing in cold water.

An Indian ink drawing may now be made upon this blue photographic print, and sent for process without the necessity of bleaching, because blue will not reproduce. If, on the other hand, it is desired to see the drawing as black lines upon white paper, the blue print may be bleached out in a few seconds by immersing it in a dish of water in which a small piece of what chemists call carbonate of soda (common washing soda) has been dissolved.

Outline drawings for reproduction by process may be made upon tracing-paper. Most of the rough illustrations and portrait sketches printed in the morning and evening newspapers are tracings made in this way from photographs or from other more elaborate illustrations. Although this is not at all a dignified branch of art, yet some of the little portrait heads that appear from time to time in the *St. James's Gazette*, *Pall Mall Gazette*, and the *Westminster Gazette* are models of selection and due economy of line, calculated to give all the essentials of portraiture, while having due regard to the exigencies of the newspaper printing press.

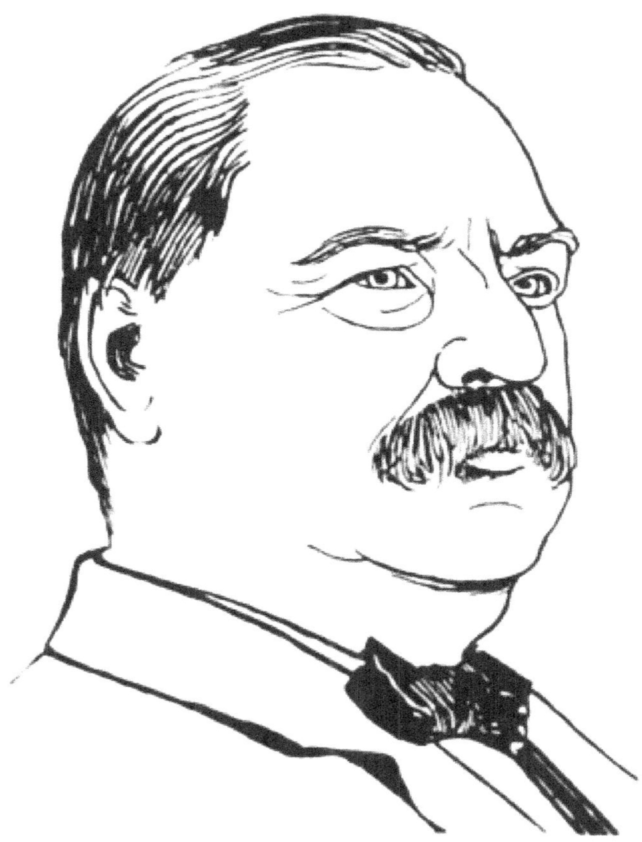

The two outline portrait sketches shown here are reproduced from the *St. James's Gazette*. Their thick lines have a tendency to become offensive when subjected to careful book-printing, but appearing as they originally did in the rapidly printed editions of an evening paper, this emphasis of line was exactly suited to the occasion.

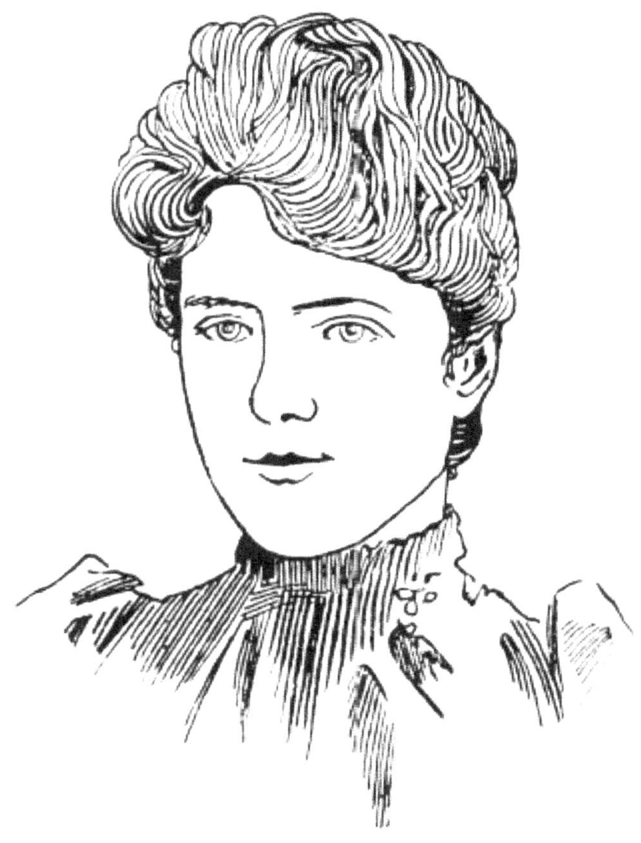

Translucent white tracing-paper should be used for tracing purposes, pinned securely through the corners of the photograph or drawing to be copied in this manner on to a drawing-board, so that the tracing may not be shifted while in progress. No pencilling is necessary, but the tracing should be made in ink, straight away. Fixed Indian ink should be used, because when the tracing is finished it will be necessary for process purposes to paste it upon cardboard, and, tracing-paper being so thin, the moisture penetrates, and would smudge a drawing made in soluble inks unless the very greatest care was taken. Old tracing-paper which has turned a yellow colour should on no account be used, and tracing-cloth is rarely available, because, although beautifully transparent, it is generally too greasy for pure line-work.

Pen-drawings which are to be made and reproduced for the newspaper press at the utmost speed are made upon lithographic transfer paper in lithographic ink, a stubborn and difficult material of a fatty nature. Drawings made in this way are not photographed, but transferred direct to the zinc plate, and etched in a very short space of time. No reduction in scale is possible, and the original drawing is inevitably destroyed in the process of transferring.

WASH DRAWINGS.

Wash drawings for reproduction by half-tone process should be made upon smooth or finely grained cardboards. Reeves' London board is very good for the purpose, and so is a French board they keep, stamped in the corner of each sheet with the initials A. L. in a circle. Wash drawings should be made in different gradations of the same colour if a good result is to be expected: thus a wash drawing in lampblack should be executed only in shades of lampblack, and not varied by the use of sepia in some parts, or of Payne's grey in others. Lampblack is a favourite material, and excellent from the photographic point of view. Payne's grey, or neutral tint, at one time had a great vogue, but it is too blue in all its shades for altogether satisfactory reproduction, although the illustration, _The Houses of Parliament_, shown on p. 122, has come well with its use. Chinese white was freely used in the drawing, and its value is shown in putting in the swirls of fog.

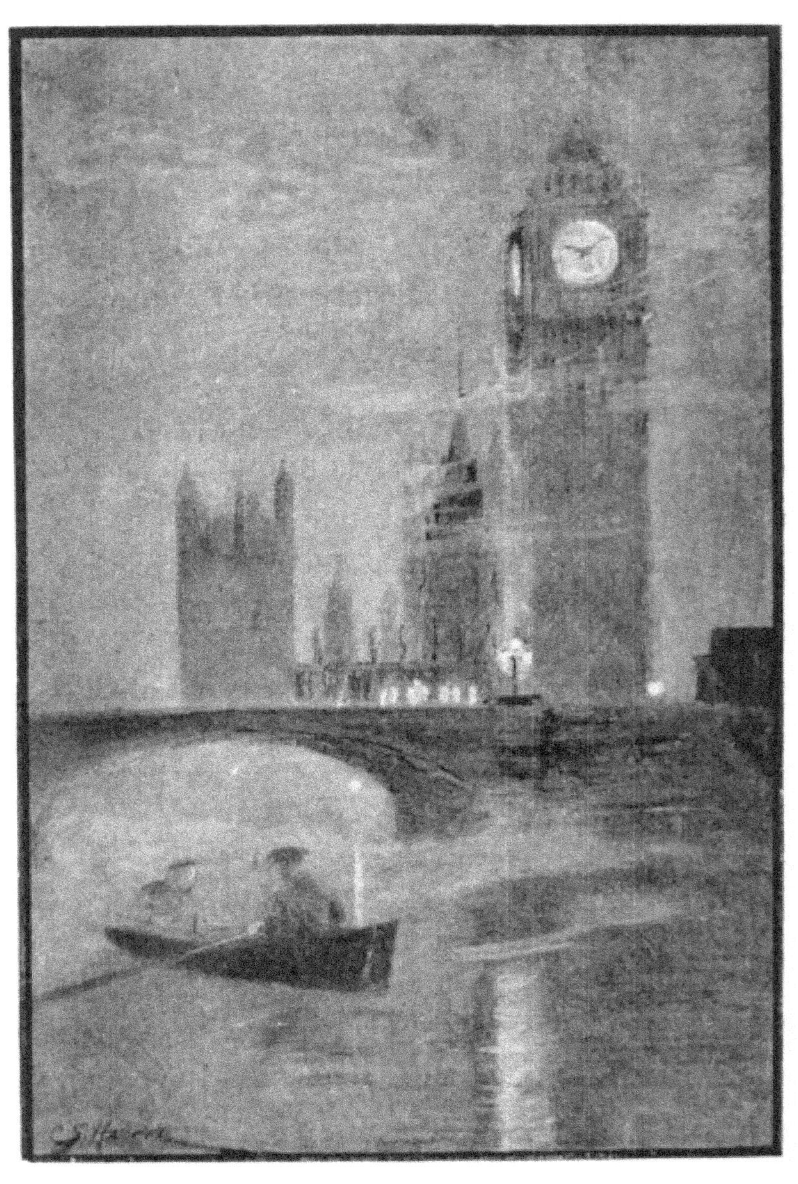

11½ × 17½.   THE HOUSES OF PARLIAMENT AT NIGHT,

FROM THE RIVER.

Wash drawing in Payne's grey.
Half-tone process, medium grain.

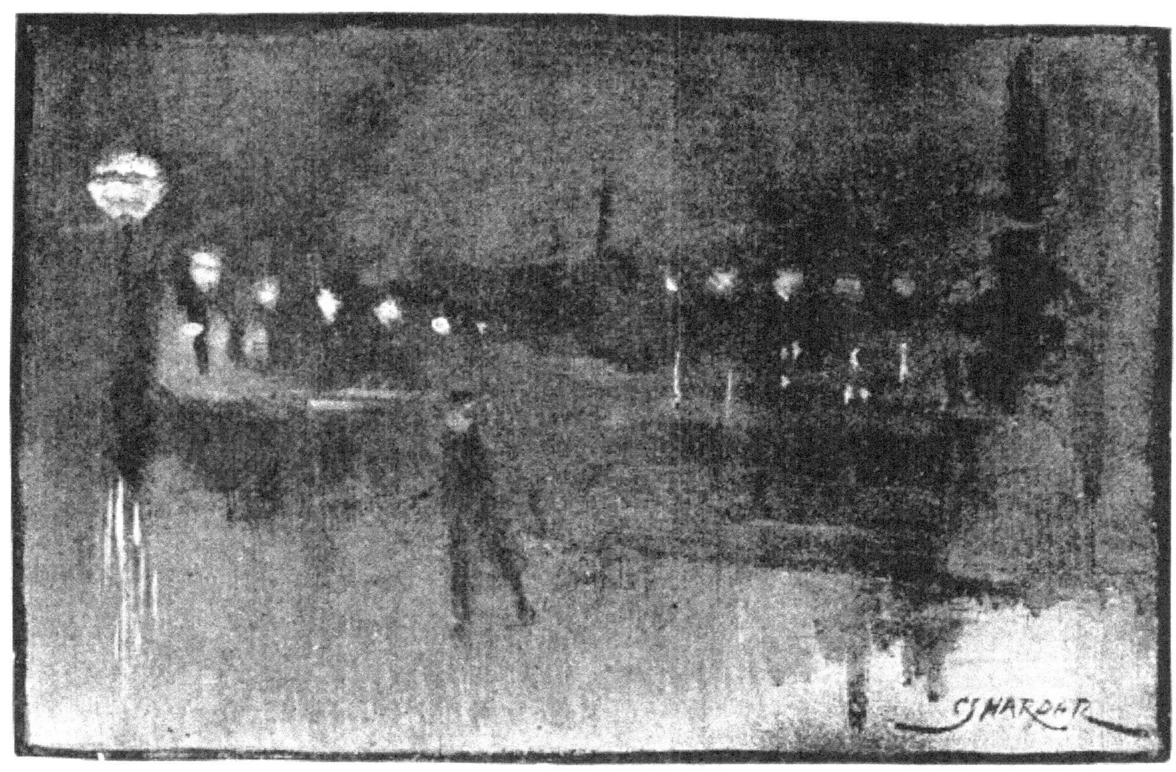

5¾ × 3¾. VICTORIA EMBANKMENT NEAR BLACKFRIARS BRIDGE:

A FOGGY NIGHT.

Drawing on paper in charcoal-grey, lights put in with Chinese white. Medium grain.

Indian ink is capable of producing the greatest range of tone from light to dark, and successive washes with it are quite indelible. But it may be said at once that this great range is not necessary—nay, is not advisable in drawing for half-tone reproduction. In view of the unavoidable defects of the half-tone processes which tend to flatten out the picture, artists should not attempt many and delicate gradations. Half a dozen tones from black to white will generally suffice. Any attempt to secure the thousand-and-one gradations of a photograph will be at once needless and harmful.

Pure transparent water-colour washes do not give such good effects in reproduction as work in body-colour. Chinese white mixed with lampblack comes beautifully. Charcoal-grey, of recent introduction, is not so well adapted to the admixture of body-colour. Altogether, charcoal-grey, although a very admirable colour, is a difficult material unless you know exactly at starting a drawing what you intend to do. The illustration, _Victoria Embankment: a Foggy Night_, was made in it on rough paper. The nature of the subject rendered the execution of the drawing easy, but in a drawing which runs the whole gamut of tone, its unstable qualities forbid its use by the novice.

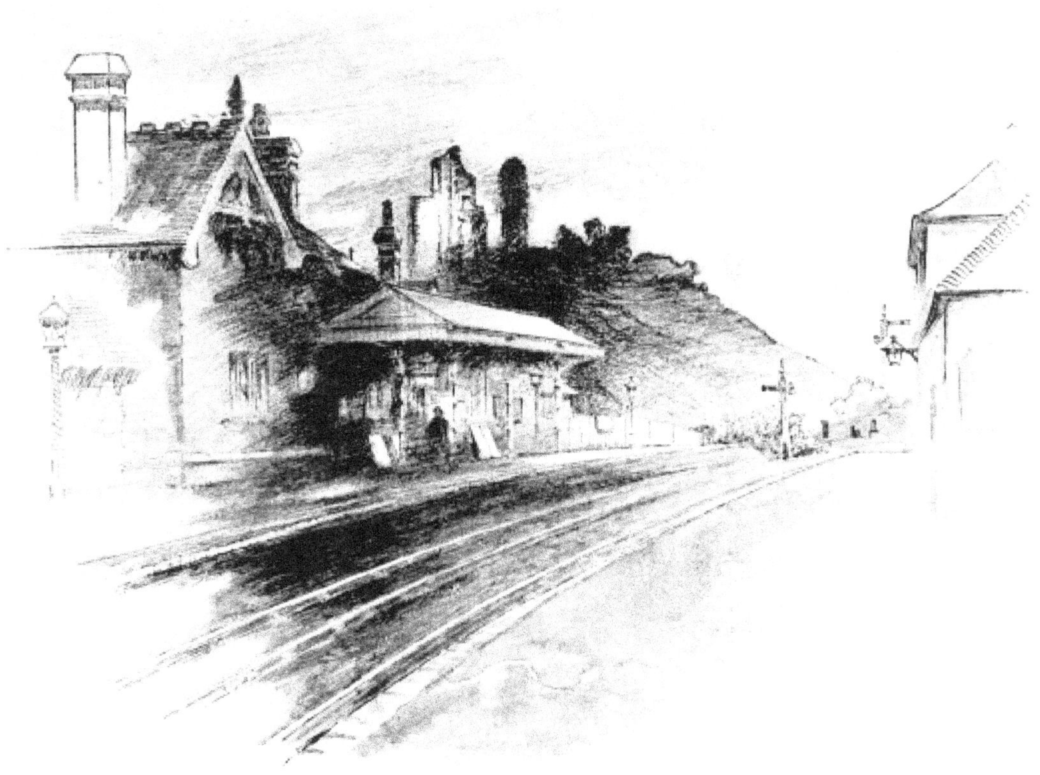

13 × 10.   CORFE RAILWAY STATION.

_Drawing upon common rough scribbling paper in Indian ink,
washes reinforced by pencil lines. Fine grain._

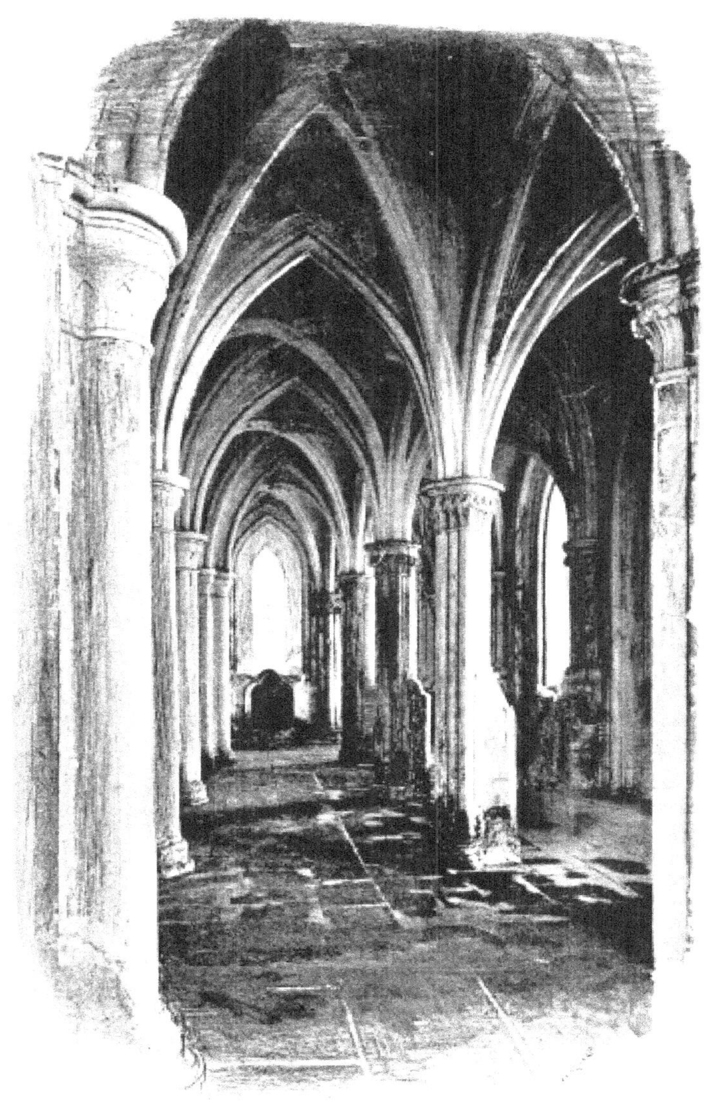

10½ × 6½. THE AMBULATORY, DORE ABBEY.

Photograph painted in parts with body-colour.

The drawings made in wash by Myrbach and Rossi have set the fashion for much recent illustration. Vignettes made with a full brush and reduced to infinitesimal proportions have abounded since the illustrated editions of *Tartarin of Tarascon* first charmed the eye; but now, reduced to the common denominator of the sixpenny magazines, they have lost all the qualities and retained all the defects the fashion ever had. The drawing of *Corfe Railway Station* was made in washes of Indian ink with a full brush, each successive wash left to dry thoroughly before the next was laid on.

Parts are reinforced with pencil strokes: these can readily be identified in the print. The block was then vignetted.

Another method is used for half-tone work. A photograph is mounted upon cardboard, and may be worked upon in brushwork with body-colour to any extent, either for lightening the picture or for making it darker. For working upon the ordinary silver-print an admixture of ox-gall must be used or the pigments will not "take" upon the sensitized paper.[1] The illustration, _The Ambulatory, Dore Abbey,_ is from a photograph, worked upon in this manner. The photo was so dark and indefinite that something was necessary to be done to show the springing of the arches and the relation of one pier to another. Chinese white was used in the manner described above, and the arches outlined in places by scratching with the sharp point of a penknife.

[1] Refer to _The Real Japan,_ by Henry Norman. Fisher Unwin, 1892. The book is freely illustrated with half-tone blocks made from photographs. The photographs were all extensively worked upon with body-colour in this manner. Indeed, the brushwork may clearly be discerned in the reproductions.

Tinted cards may be used in drawing for half-tone, but yellow tints must be avoided, for obvious photographic reasons; and blue tints, photographically, are practically pure white. If tinted cardboard is used at all, it should be in tints of grey or brown.

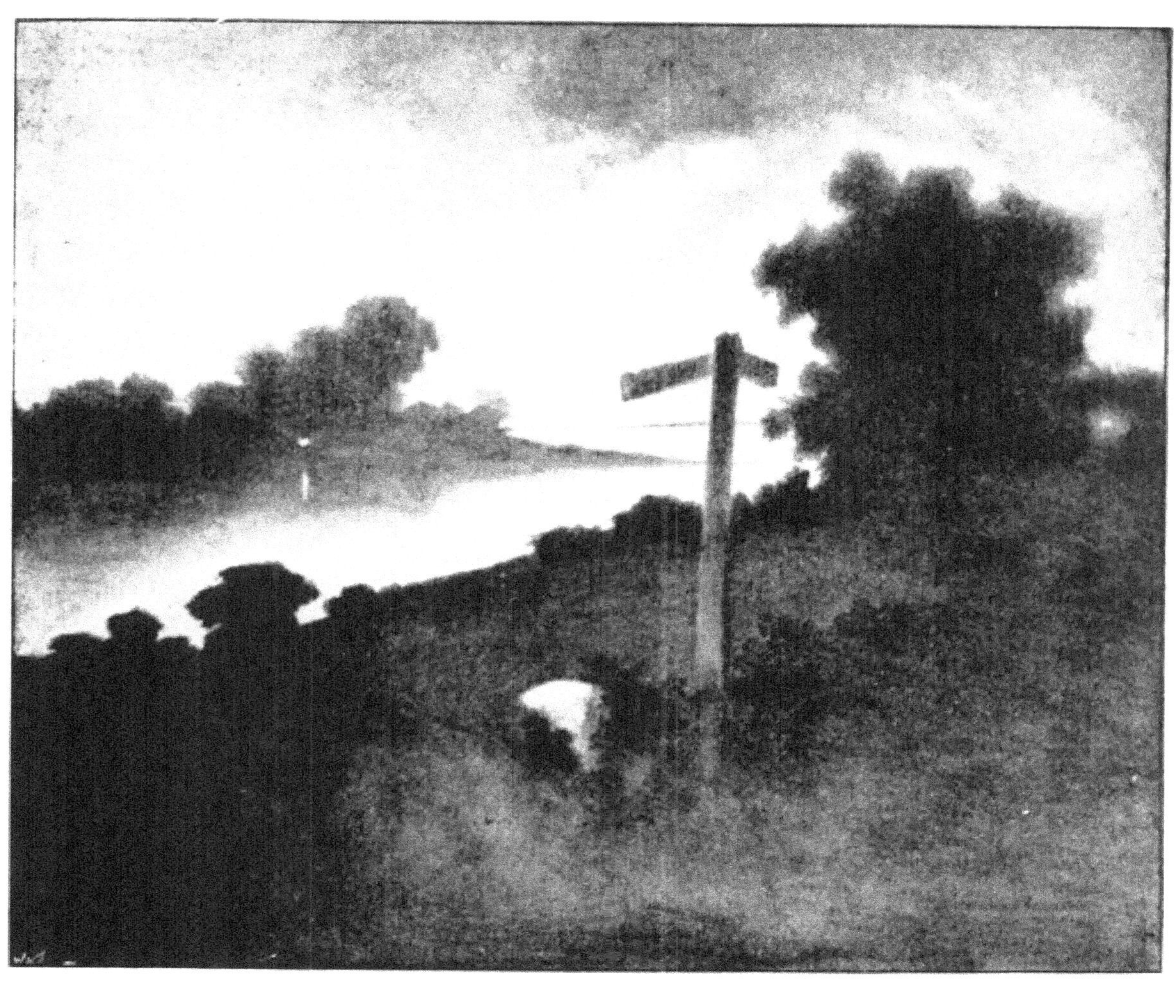

14 × 12.   MOONLIGHT: CONFLUENCE OF THE SEVERN AND
THE WYE.

Oil sketch on canvas in Payne's grey. Half-tone process. Fine grain.

A very satisfactory way of working for half-tone is to work in oil monochrome. The reproductions from oil sketches come very well indeed by half-tone processes: full and vigorous. The photo-engraver always objects to oil because of its gloss, but this can be obviated by mixing your colour with turpentine or benzine, which give a dull surface. The sketch shown on p. 130 was made in this way. It was a smoothly worked sketch, with no aggressive brush-marks, but it may be noted that brush-marks come beautifully by this process: if anything, rather stronger than in the original, because the shadows cast by them reproduce as well. But if you sketch in oils for reproduction, be chary of vigorous brushwork in white: it comes unpleasantly prominent in the block.

In giving instructions for the reproduction, and reduction, of drawings, the measurement in one direction of the reproduction desired should be plainly indicated thus: ← 4½ inches →. Unless absolutely unavoidable, drawings should not be sent marked "½ size," "⅓ scale," and so on, because these terms are apt to mislead. People not accustomed to measurements are very uncertain in their understanding of them, and, absurd as it may seem to those who deal in mensuration, they very frequently take ½ scale and ½ size as synonymous terms; while ½ scale is really ¼ size, and so on, in proportion.

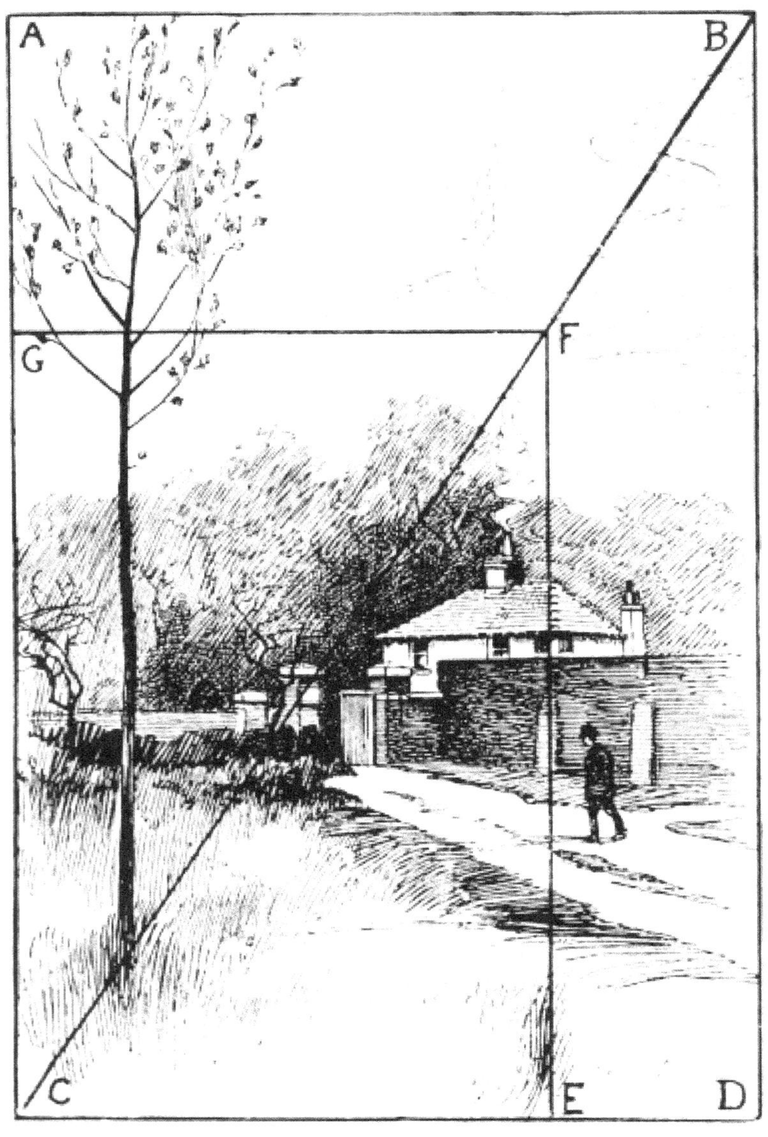

The proportions a drawing will assume when reduced may be ascertained in this way. You have, say, a narrow upright drawing, as shown in the above diagram, and you want the width reduced to a certain measurement, but having marked this off are at a loss to know what height the reproduction will be. Supposing it to be a pen-drawing, vignetted, as most pen-drawings are; in the first place, light pencil lines touching the farthest projections of the drawing should be ruled to each of its four sides, meeting accurately at the angles A, B, C, D. This frame being made, a diagonal line should be lightly ruled from upper to lower corner, either—as shown—from B to C, or from A to D. The measurement of the proposed reduction should then be marked off upon the base line at E, and a perpendicular line ruled from it to meet the diagonal. The point of contact, F, gives the height that was to be found, and a horizontal line from F to G completes the diagram, and gives the correct proportions of the block to be made.

It will readily be seen that large copies of small sketches can be made in exact proportions by a further application of the diagonal, but care should be taken to have all these lines drawn scrupulously accurate, because the slightest deviation throws the proportions all out.

STYLES AND MANNER.

Pen-drawing is ruled by expediency more, perhaps, than any art. I shall not say that one method is more right than another in the management of textures, or in the elaboration or mere suggestion of detail, for line work is, to begin with, a purely arbitrary rendering of tones. There is nothing like line in nature. Take up an isolated brick; it does not suggest line in any way. Build it up with others into a wall, and you can in pen and ink render that wall in many ways that will be equally convincing and right. It may be expressed in terms of splatter-work, which can be made to represent admirably a wall where the bricks have become welded into an homogeneous mass, individually indistinguishable by age, or of vertical or horizontal lines that may or may not take account of each individual brick and the joints of the mortar that binds the courses together. Crosshatching, though a cheap expedient and a decaying convention, may be used. But to lose sight of ordinary atmospheric conditions is no more privileged in pen-work than in paint. This is not by any means unnecessary or untimely advice, though it should be. The fact of using a pen instead of a brush does not empower anybody to play tricks with the solar system, though one sees it constantly done. One continually sees in pen-drawing the laws of light and shade set at naught, and nobody says anything against it—perhaps it looks smart. Certainly the effect is novel, and novelty is a powerful factor in anything. But to draw a wall shining with a strong diffused light which throws a great black shadow, is contrary to art and nature both. "Nature," according to Mr. Whistler, "may be 'creeping up,' but she has not reached that point yet. When one sees suns setting behind the east ends of cathedrals, with other vagaries of that sort, one simply classes such things with that amusing erratum of Mr. Rider Haggard's, in which he describes a ship 'steaming out of the mouth of the Thames, shaping her course toward the red ball of the setting sun.'" But though the instance is amusing, the custom is apt to pall.

Some of the American pen-draughtsmen who contribute to the *Century* are exceedingly clever, and their handling extremely personal; but after a time this excessive personality ceases to charm, and, for one thing, these young bloods are curiously narrow in their choice of the masters from whom they are only too pleased to derive. Mr. Brennan is, perhaps, the most curiously original of these men. He is the man who has shown most convincingly that the inked thumb is the most instant and effective instrument wherewith to render velvet in a pen-drawing. You cannot fail to be struck with his method; his manner is entirely personal, and yet, after a time, it worries one into intolerance.

It is the same with that convention, founded, apparently, by Mr. Herbert Railton, which has had a long run of some nine or ten years. It was a convention in pictorial architecture that had nothing except a remarkably novel technique to recommend it. The illustrator invited us rather to see how "pretty" he could render an old building, than how nearly he could show it us as it stood. He could draw an elevation in a manner curiously feminine, but he could only repeat himself and his trees; his landscapes were insults to the imagination. Nothing inspired him to achievements beyond pictorial confectionery.

This convention has had its day, although in the mean while so strikingly mannered was it that it appealed to almost all the young and undiscriminating men whose work lay in the rendering of pictorial architecture. "Go to," said the Average Artist in "the picturesque," "I will sit down and make a drawing in the manner of Mr. Railton." And he did, generally, it may be observed, from a photograph, and in the undistracting seclusion of his own room. This sort of artistic influenza, which nearly all the younger men caught at one time or another, was very dangerous to true art. But it could not possibly last; it was so resourceless. Always we were invited to glance at the same sky and an unchanging rendering of buildings, whether old or new, in the same condition of supposedly picturesque decrepitude. Everything in this mannerism wore the romantic air of the Moated Grange and radiated Mrs. Radcliffe, dungeons, spectres, and death, whether the subject was a ruinated castle or a new warehouse. All this has grown offensive: we want more sobriety. This apotheosis of raging skies and falling smuts, of impending chimneys, crumbling stones, and tottering walls was only a personal manner. Its imitators have rendered it ridiculous.

The chief merits of such topographical and archæological drawings are that they be truthful and reverent. If art is ever to approach the documentary stage, to be used as the record of facts, it is in this matter. To flood the country with representations of old buildings that are not so much pictures of them as exercises in an exaggerated personal manner, is to deserve ill at the hands of all who would have preserved to them the appearance of places that are passing away. The illustrations to such books, say, as Mr. Loftie's *Inns of Court* or his *Westminster Abbey* are of no historic or artistic value whatever; they are merely essays in a wild and weird manner of which we are tired in the originator of it; which we loathe in those who imitate its worst faults. We require a sober style in this work, after being drunken so long with its so-called picturesqueness, which, rightly considered, is but impressionism, ill seen and uninstructed.

No one has exercised so admirable a method, whether in landscape, in portraiture, or in architecture, as Sir George Reid, but his work is not readily accessible for the study it invites. It is scholarly and expressive, eloquent of the character of his subject, free from redundancies. It is elaborate or suggestive on due occasion, and, although the style is so distinguished, you always feel that every drawing by this stylist is really and truly a representation of the person, place, or thing he has drawn, and not a mere pretext for an individual handling; no braggart assumption of "side."

The dangers of following in a slavish manner the eccentricities of well-known men are exemplified in the work of those illustrators who ape the whimsies of the impressionist Degas. What Degas may do may nearly always be informed with distinction, but the illustrators who reproduce, not his genius, but an outstanding feature of it, are singularly narrow. If Degas has painted a picture of the play with the orchestra in the foreground and the bass-viol looming immensely up three parts of the composition, the third-rate impressionists also lug in a bass-viol; if he has shown a ballet-girl with apparently only one leg, they always draw one-legged *coryphées*, and remain incapable of conceiving them as bipeds.

Caldecott is a dangerous man to copy. He was, first and last, a draughtsman, and a draughtsman whose every dot and line were eloquent. There is no technique that you can lay hold of in his work, but only characterization, which is more frequently caricature. Caldecott would never have made a serious illustrator; in burlesque he was immense, and no artist could desire a better monument than his *Picture Books*. His reputation has fallen greatly of late, notwithstanding the delightful *John Gilpin* and the others of that inimitable series; but his repute had stood higher to-day if his private letters to his friends and other unconsidered trifles had never been collected and published, ghoul-like, after his death. Pandering to the market has almost killed Caldecott's repute, for the undiscriminating public were invited to admire reproductions of hasty sketches never intended for publicity.

There is character in Mr. Phil May's work, and humour, surprisingly set forth with a marvellous economy of line. His is a gay and festive muse, that is most at home where the tide of life runs strongest and deepest, with wine-bubbles breaking "most notoriously," as Mr. Kipling might say, upon its surface; with theatres, music-halls, and Gaiety bars ranged along its banks in profusion. There is much human nature in Mr. May. Also in Mr. Greiffenhagen; but a different kind. He has gone chiefly to the boudoir and the drawing-room for his subjects, and has rendered them with a resolute impressionism and a thorough discarding of cross-hatch that make a lasting impression with the beholder. There is a certain Christmas number, 1892, of the *Lady's Pictorial* with memorable drawings by him; they are in wash and lithographic crayon, but may only be noted here in passing. He has a gift of novel, unhackneyed composition, and he sees the figure for himself, and draws it in with a daring but right and striking manner.

There has arisen of late years a school of illustration peculiarly English—the so to call it "Decorative School." It is a new and higher incarnation of the pre-Raphaelite movement. The brotherhood did good work, not at all commensurate with the amount of attention it received, but beyond all praise in the conventions it founded; and, historically considered, Rossetti and his fellows are great, and Blake is greater, because he was an inspired visionary with a kink in his brain, out of which flowed imaginings the most gorgeous and original. But the decorative men of to-day are doing even better work—masculine, convincing, racy of this soil. It is chiefly admirable because it gives us, in these days of "actuality," of photography, and reproductions direct from photographs, a new outlook upon life. English decorative illustration is, with but few exceptions, possessed of a fine romantic fancy, poetic, and at the same time healthy and virile and eminently sane, and it will live. There is great hope for the future of this school, while the imported styles of Vierge and Rico and other masters used to sunnier skies, admirable beyond expression in their own places, droop and languish in the nor'-easterly winds of England, and their tradition becomes attenuated in passing through so many hands. Their descendants, from Abbey down to Pennell and the whole crowd of those who love not wisely but too well, have brought these fine exotic conventions down to the merest shadows of shades.

Mr. Walter Crane has, any time these last ten years, been the great Apostle of Decoration *plus* Socialism. It has been given him in this wise to make (in theory) the lion to lie down with the lamb (and yet for the lamb to remain outside the lion with his destiny of mutton still in perspective), and he has proclaimed in parables the possibility of mixing oil and water. He has perpetrated a cartoon for the Socialistic, if not Anarchist, First of May, and therein he has striven to decoratively treat the British Workman. But although Mr. Crane has a pretty trick of decoration, he was worsted in that bout, for the British Plumber or the Irish Hodman is stubborn material for decoration, and their spouses as festal nymphs are not convincing visions. Again, he has achieved a weird series of cartoons upon the walls of the Red Cross Hall in praise of Democratic Valour, in which he has unsuccessfully attempted to conventionalize rescuing firemen and heroic police. Such bravery deserved a better fate. Also Mr. Crane has written much revolutionary verse in praise of brotherhood and equality, and now he has accepted the mastership of a Governmental art school, under the direction of that not very revolutionary body, the Committee of Council for Education (Science and Art Department). Decoration should be made of sterner stuff! His industry has been prodigious. Even now a bibliography of him is in the making; and yet shall it be said that it is difficult in the great mass of his work to find many items altogether satisfactory? It may be feared it is so. For one thing, his anatomy is habitually at fault; and yet has he not informed an interviewer from the *Pall Mall Gazette* that long years since he had ceased to draw from the model?

That wheel within wheels, the so-called Birmingham School, is attracting attention just now, and men begin to prophesy of deeds from out the midlands. But once upon a time there was a Newlyn School, was there not? Where is that party now? Its foremost members have won to the honours of the Royal Academy, and its mission is done. But it is time to talk of schools when work has been done. Of course it is very logical that good work should come from Birmingham. The sense of beauty is stronger in those who live in midst of dirt and grime. Instance the Glasgow school of impressionists. But the evidence of Birmingham at present is but a touching follow-on to the styles of Mr. Crane and Mr. Sumner, and to the ornament of Mr. Lewis Day. Indeed, the decorative work of the students at the National Art Training Schools may be put in the formula of one-third Crane, and the remaining two-thirds Heywood Sumner and Lewis Day, an amalgam ill-considered and poorly wrought.

But indeed Mr. Heywood Sumner's work has a note of distinction. He does not confuse Socialist propaganda with ornament, and is not always striving to show with emphasis of line in pen and ink that Capital is the natural enemy of Labour, and that a silk hat on a rich man's head may justly be defined as so many loaves of bread (or pots of beer) in the wrong place. That is for Mr. Crane and Mr. William Morris to prove; and, really, anything wicked can be proven of such a hideous object. But the onus of bringing the guilt home to it and the wearer of it does not produce good art. Indeed, decorative art is not catholic; it has no sort of commerce with everyday life or with the delineation of any times so recent as the early years of the Victorian era. Its field lies only in poetic imaginings, in fancy, and, most emphatically, not in fact. When Mr. Crane, for instance, takes to idealising the heroic acts of policemen, the impulse does credit to his heart, but the results are not flattering to his head. Fortunately he does not often go these lengths, and no one else of the decorative idea has been equally courageous, save indeed a Mr. Beardsley, who "decoratively" illustrated Orpheus at the Lyceum Theatre; and those illustrations in the *Pall Mall Budget*, March 16, 1893, certainly were very dreadful.

An exception to the general beauty of recent decorative work is the incomprehensible and at the same time unlovely practice of this eccentric. Mr. Charles Ricketts' work, although its meaning may often be so subtly symbolical that it is not to be understood except by the elect,—never without the aid of a glossary of symbolism,—is always graced with interesting technicalities, and his draughtsmanship is of the daintiest; but what of meaning is conveyed to the mind and what of beauty to the eye in this work of Mr. Beardsley's, that has been somewhat spoken of lately? It has imagination certainly, but morbid and neurotic, with a savour of Bethlehem Hospital and the charnel-house; it is eccentric apparently with an eccentricity that clothes bad draughtsmanship, and incongruous with an incongruity that suggests the uninstructed enthusiasm of the provincial mind. It exhibits a patchwork-quilt kind of eclecticism, born of a fleeting glance at Durer; of a nodding acquaintance with all prominent modern decoration and an irrelevant *soupçon* of Renaissance ornament; like the work of a lithographic draughtsman, a designer of bill-heads, roaming fancy free.

The practice of Mr. Selwyn Image has a devotional and meditative cast. He has made some remarkable drawings for the *Hobby Horse* in the manner of the missal-painters, both in spirit and execution, and he steadfastly keeps the art of the monkish scriptorium in view, and seems to echo the sentiments of the rapturous maidens in *Patience*, "Let us be Early English ere it is too late." And he *is* Early English to excellent purpose.

It is a gross error to hold that decorative art is impossible under present social conditions, and unpardonable to attempt to link decoration and design to Socialist propaganda. Art of all possible application never flourished so well as under the feudal system, and never sank so low as it did when Democracy and the Trouser came in together.

The great advantages of Art over Photography are its personal qualities. The camera is impersonal, and will ever be a scientific instrument. You can, like the ingenious Mr. H. P. Robinson, pose figures, and with a combination of negatives concoct a composition which is some sort of cousin-german to a picture; but if you can do all this, you might go a little farther and make a picture without the aid of a camera. It would be personal, and, without a signature, signed all over with the unmistakable mark of style or manner, like Constable's paintings.

It seems unlikely that any mechanical processes, save the strictly autographic, which reproduce line, will be of permanent artistic value. No photogravure will be sought for and prized in years to come as the old etchings and mezzotints are valued. Those elaborate photogravure plates from popular or artistic pictures (the terms are not synonymous) which crowd the print-sellers' shops to-day, at five or ten guineas, will not long hence be accounted dear at so many shillings, simply because they lack the personal note. Meanwhile, mezzotints and etchings, other than the "commercial" etching, will become inversely expensive.

In that brackish flood of "bitter cries" to which we have been subjected of late years, the wail of the wood-engraver was easily to be distinguished, and we heard that his occupation was gone. But has it? No, nor will it go. No tint nor half-tone process can ever render sufficiently well the wash drawings that the best engravers render so admirably, with an entire subjection of their own individuality unthought of twenty years ago. The wood-engraver, as one who imposes restrictions upon technique, has had his day; but as a conscientious and skilful workman, who renders faithfully the personality of the artist he engraves, he flourishes, and will continue to flourish. Otherwise, there is no hope for him, let Mr. Linton say what he will. He will remain because he can preserve the personal note.

Half-tone processes are as tricky as Puck and as inconstant. You never know the exact result you will get from any given drawing. Half a dozen blocks from the same drawing will give, each one, a different result, because so much depends upon the fraction of a second, more or less, in making the negative; but all of them agree in presenting an aspect similar to that obtained on looking through the wire blind of some Philistine window upon the street. In all cases the edge, the poignancy of the subject, is taken off, and, in the case of the process-block, several intermediate tones go as well, with, frequently, the result of an unnatural lighting "that never was on land or sea," and it may be hoped never will be.

No doubt half-tone processes will continue to be more and more widely used, chiefly because they are several times cheaper than a good wood engraving, and because, so far as mere documentary evidence goes, they are good enough for illustrated journalism. But for bookwork, for anything that is not calculated for an ephemeral consideration, half-tone processes are only to be used with the most jealous care.

As regards the half-tone processes employed to reproduce photographs, I take leave to say that no one will, a hundred years hence, prize them for any quality. The necessary reticulation of their surface subtracts from them something of the documentary value of the photograph, and, deriving directly from photographs, they have no personal or artistic interest.

But their present use touches the professional draughtsman nearly, for in illustrated journalism half-tone is very frequently used in reproducing photographs of places and people without the aid of the artist, and it is no consolation for a man who finds his occupation going for him to consider that these direct photographic processes have no permanent interest. It is the new version of the old tale of the stage-coach *versus* the railway engine, to his mind, and he is apt to think that as a craftsman he is fast following the wood-engraver. But it is safe to say that although the mediocrities will suffer, or be forced, like the miniature-painter who turned daguerrotypist and then blossomed forth as a photographer, to study practical evolution, the artists of style and distinction will rather gain than lose by a further popularity of cheap photographic blocks. The illustrated papers and magazines will not be so freely open to them as before, but in the illustration of books will lie their chief field, and who knows but that by such a time the pen-drawing and the drawing in wash will have won at last to the picture-frame and the art galleries. There's distinction for you!

So much to show the value of personality.

Still it remains that, although the personal element will always be valued, the fact—to paraphrase a sounding Ruskinian anathema—gives no reason for flinging your identity in the face of your contemporaries, or even of posterity (this last a long shot which few, with all the will in the world, will be able to achieve). You may be startlingly original and brilliant in technique, and be received with the acclaim that always awaits a novelty; but if your personality be so exaggerated that you allow it to override the due presentment of your subject, why, then, your plaudits will not be of very long continuance.

PAINTERS' PEN-DRAWINGS.

It is to the painters that we owe some curious and original effects in pen-drawing, that no professional pen-draughtsman who has studied the science of reproduction could have given us, however independent his attitude towards process.

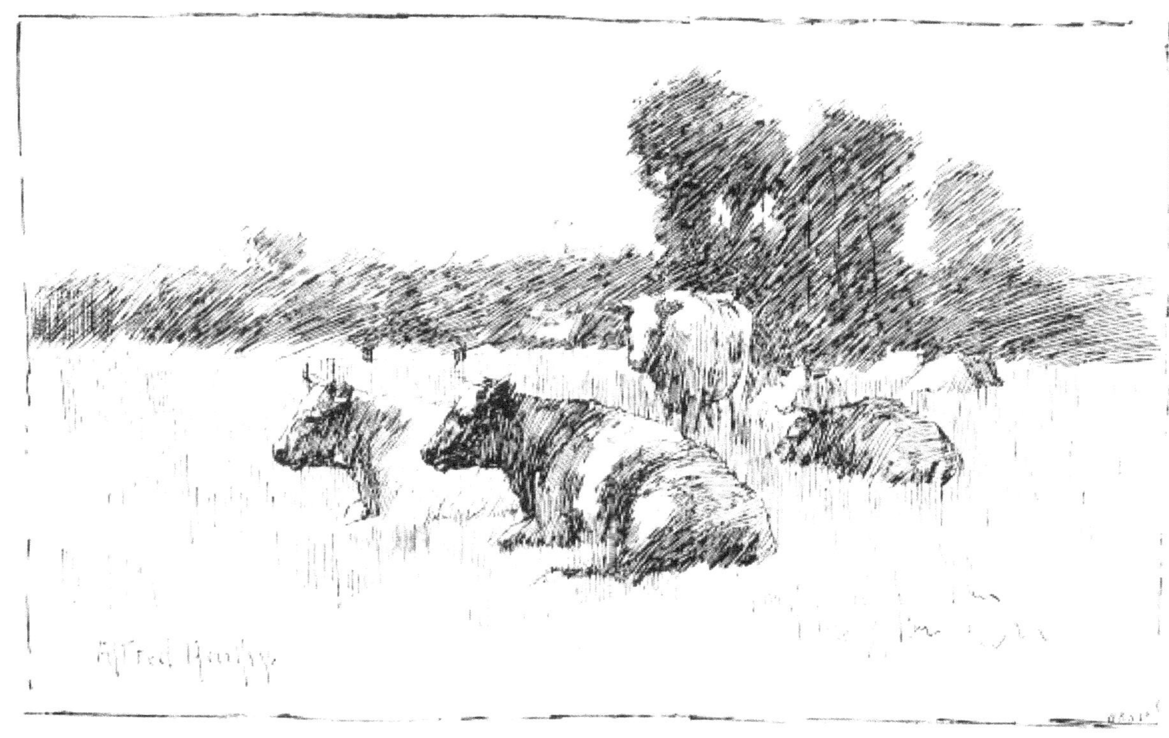

7¾ × 5.   PASTURAGE.

From a drawing by Mr. Alfred Hartley.

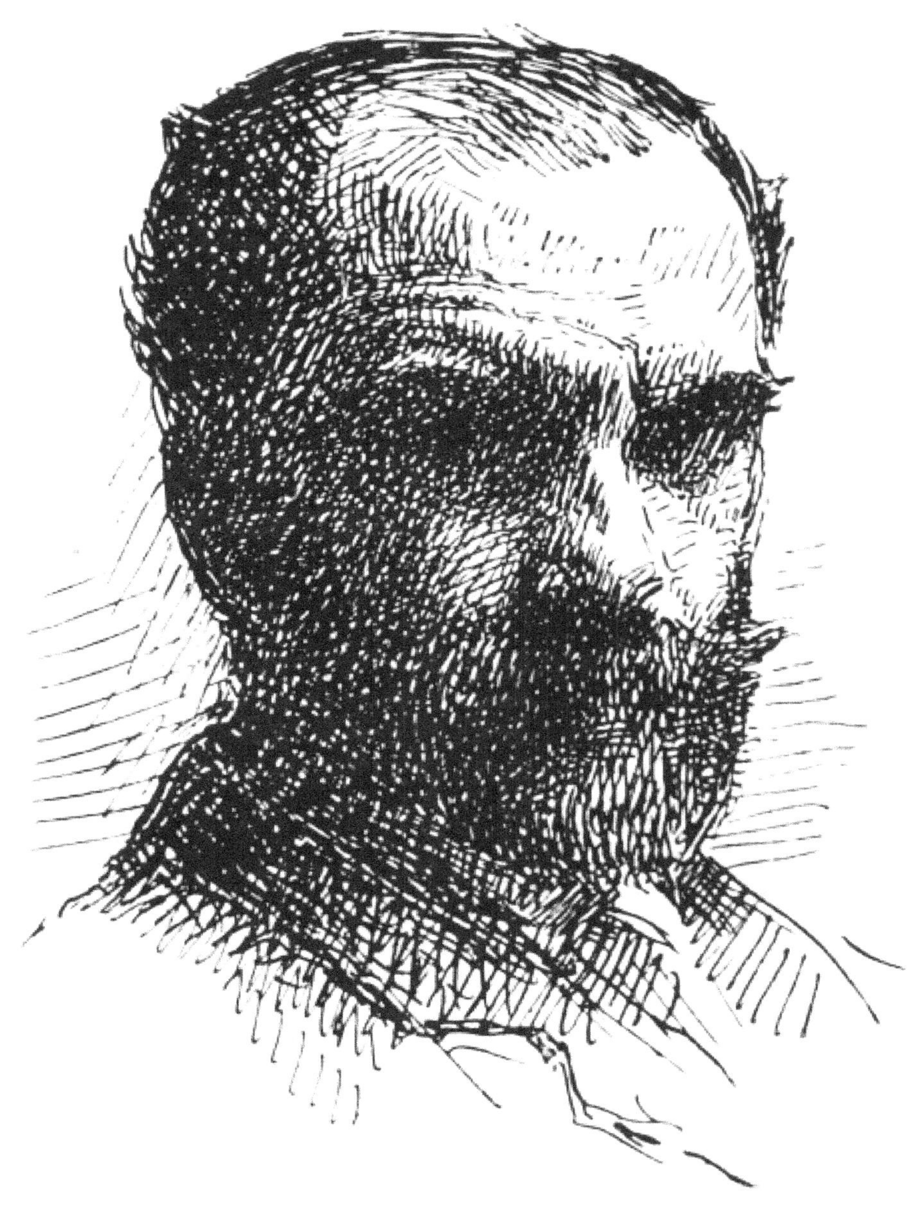

PORTRAIT OF MR. BONNAT, BY HIMSELF.

Painters who have known nothing whatever of processes have from time to time been called upon to make pen-drawings from their paintings for reproduction in illustrated exhibition catalogues, and their drawings have frequently been both of the most ludicrously impossible character from the process point of view, and bad from the independent penman's standpoint. But a percentage of this painters' pen-work, done as it was with a free hand and an unprejudiced brain, is curiously instructive. A very great number of painters' pen-drawings have been made up to within the last few years (since which time half-tone process blocks produced from photos of their pictures have superseded them), and painters have in no small measure helped to advance the science of process-work, merely by reason of the difficulty of reproducing their drawings adequately, and the consequent renewed efforts of the process-man toward the adequate translation of their frequently untranslateable qualities. The graver has been pressed into the service of process partly on their account, and the roulette has been used freely to assuage the crudities resulting on the block from drawings utterly unsuitable for straight-away processing.

In this connection half-tone processes have done inestimable harm, for, to-day, the catalogues and the illustrated papers are filled with photographic reproductions of paintings where in other days autographic sketches by the painters themselves were used to give a value that is now lacking to these records of exhibitions.

They have frequently a heavy hand, these painters, and are prodigal of their ink; moreover, they have not the paralyzing dread of an immaculate sheet of white cardboard that seizes upon the black-and-white man (so to call the illustrator), who is brought up with the fear of the process-man before him.

Thus you will find Mr. Wyllie make pen-sketches from his pictures with a masterful hand, and a pen (apparently a quill) that plumbs the deepest depths of the inkpot, and produces a robustious drawing that wrings conviction out of one by the thickness and surety of its lines; or again, Mr. Blake Wirgman shows equal vigour and directness with portraits in pen-and-ink, replicas in little of his oil-paintings. One could desire nothing more masculine than the accompanying illustration from his hand.

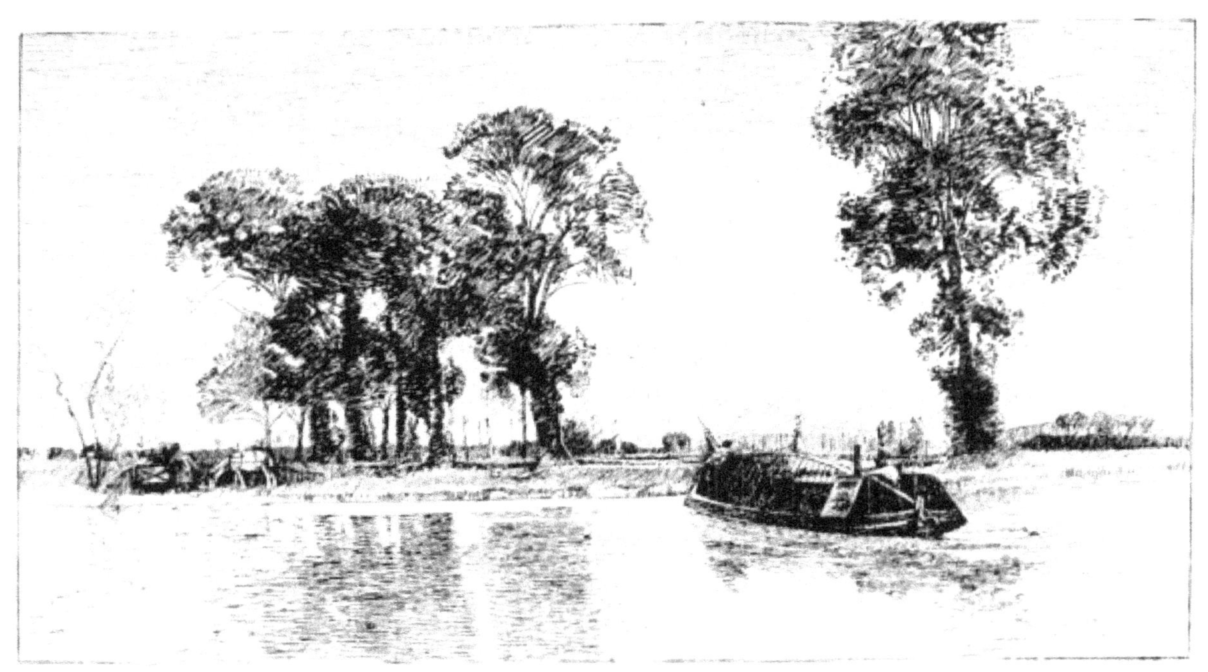

18 × 10½.   TOWING PATH,
ABINGDON.

From a drawing by Mr. David Murray.

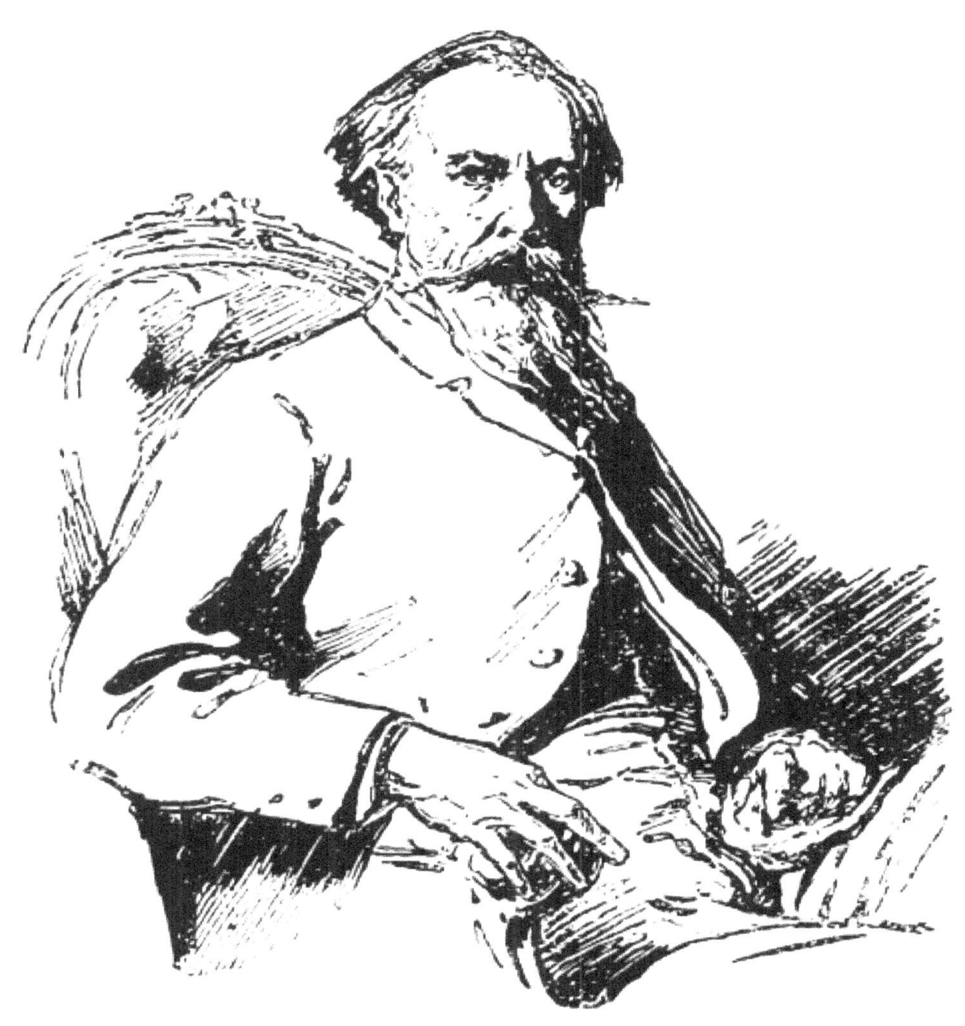

A PORTRAIT FROM A DRAWING BY MR. T. BLAKE WIRGMAN.

A striking exception to these is seen in <u>Mr. Alfred Hartley's drawing of a pasturage</u>. It is full of tender, pearly greys, and is drawn with the lightest of hands, but with a peculiar disposition of pen-strokes that no professional pen-draughtsman would employ, because of his constant care to give the process-man the easiest of problems. And the autocrat of the rocking-bath and the etching-room would veto such work as this; yet, you will observe, it comes excellently well by the ordinary zinc processes.

But with <u>Mr. David Murray's large pen-drawing</u> it was another matter. The greyness of the ink with which it was drawn and the extreme tenuity of its lines rendered it impossible of adequate reproduction except by the swelled gelatine process which has been employed. The result is admirable; all the fine grey lines in the sky are reproduced and give an excellent effect.

The <u>portrait of the painter, Mr. Bonnat, by himself</u>, is one of the most suggestive pen-drawings that can be found anywhere. It shows what admirable effects of light and shade and modelling can be obtained even with the heavy hand, and it is worthy careful study.

Unfortunately the illustrations in the long series of *Academy Notes*, in which so many autographic sketches by painters appear, are almost useless for study and comparison, because of the extreme reduction to which they have been subjected. This is greatly to be deplored, for the tendency of the times is more and more towards drawing for the limitations of process, not only in journalism, but in the more permanent illustrations of magazines and books. All this tends to bring about a hard and formal line, to establish a dry and unsatisfactory academic manner, of which the painter's pen sketches are the very antithesis. It is always well to remember that the only valid reason why process should live is that it enables the draughtsman to live his life at first hand; that is the first and last argument in favour of modern methods of reproduction.

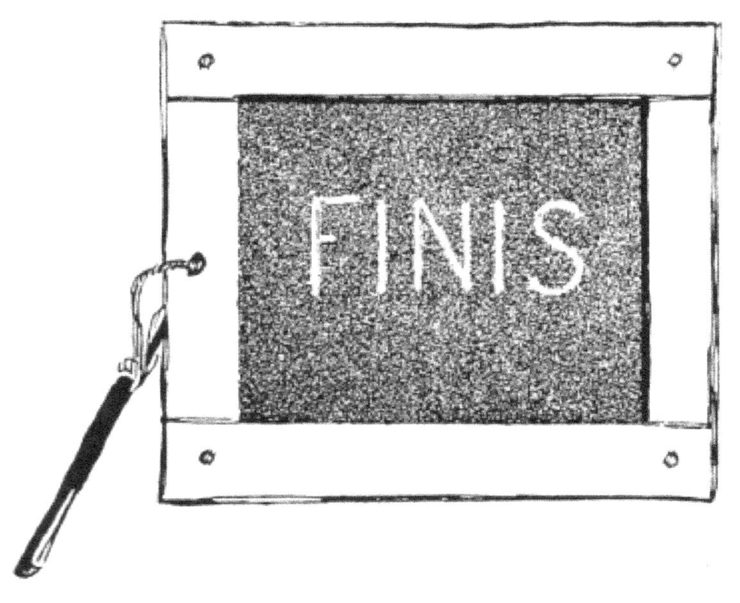